Decolonial Media Imaginaries

Decolonial Media Imaginaries

Ian Reilly

intellect
Bristol, UK / Chicago, USA

First published in the UK in 2026 by
Intellect, The Mill, Parnall Road, Fishponds, Bristol, BS16 3JG, UK

First published in the USA in 2026 by
Intellect, The University of Chicago Press, 1427 E. 60th Street,
Chicago, IL 60637, USA

EU GPSR Authorised Representative
LOGOS EUROPE, 9 rue Nicolas Poussin, 17000, LA ROCHELLE, France
E-mail: Contact@logoseurope.eu

A catalogue record for this book is available from the British Library.

Copy editor: MPS Limited
Cover designer: Natalie Thomas
Cover image: Mathew Borrett, *Hypnagogic City*, 2017.
Production manager: Tian Greaves
Typesetting: MPS Limited

Hardback ISBN 978-1-83595-238-2
Paperback ISBN 978-1-83595-358-7
ePUB ISBN 978-1-83595-239-9
ePDF ISBN 978-1-83595-240-5

To find out about all our publications, please visit our website.
There you can subscribe to our e-newsletter, browse or download our current catalogue and buy any titles that are in print.

www.intellect.com

This is a peer-reviewed publication.

To my dear parents, Julie and Greg Reilly

Contents

Figures

Preface

In January 2020, I co-organized a reading group dedicated to the writings of British-Australian feminist scholar, Sara Ahmed. Our weekly gatherings represented an opportunity for cross-disciplinary dialogue and discussion among university students and faculty in an environment that encouraged friendly and supportive exchanges. The format was so successful that the group continued beyond the initial scope of the four proposed Ahmed books[1] to encompass a much broader range of feminist texts. As the COVID-19 pandemic produced an unending wave of uncertainties, our small group became something of a lifeline for members seeking comfort, camaraderie, inspiration, and perhaps even some semblance of routine. The group-selected readings reflected a desire to engage with contemporary issues and themes that were being all the more foregrounded and exacerbated during the pandemic: precarious labour, institutional critique, Black feminist thought, emancipation struggles, decolonial feminism, Indigenous sovereignty, and abolitionism, among many others. The practice of reading together represented the possibility of decelerating, slowing things down, nurturing exchange, and building a shared set of references and vocabulary. The group modelled a feminist ethics of care that created room for members to choose a level of engagement conducive to their respective contexts and living situations. The undeniable ethos of care that informed our interactions and exchanges also laid the groundwork for the reading group to read brilliantly difficult, challenging, and unsettling works. Although our interests and concerns could certainly diverge or differ, our weekly discussions would invoke many of the following touchstones: Black Lives Matter (BLM), the Truth and Reconciliation Commission (TRC) Report's Calls to Action, Missing and Murdered Indigenous Women and Girls (MMIWG), the recovery of unmarked children's graves at former residential school sites, and various aspects of the pandemic. The cyclical and almost elliptical ways in which these themes would inform our discussions would influence not only what we would read over time, it would also incite many of us to engage in deeper reflections on our respective subjectivities, positionalities, and ethico-political commitments. What's more, the praxis of reading together prompted critical reappraisals of our professional disciplinary boundaries, offering us some leeway to distance and/or reorient ourselves away from undesirable investments in conventional disciplinarity. In my discipline – communication and media studies – calls to intervene on questions of race, inequality, and exclusion have circulated widely (Chakravartty et al. 2018; Hirji et al. 2020; Ng et al. 2020), with attention given to the troubling ubiquity and dominance of whiteness in the academy. As one recent study has shown, communication studies scholarship has been dominated over the past twenty years by a group of 1675 highly cited scholars, of which 91.5 per cent of this 'communication citation elite' (CCE) are white, 74.3 per cent are male, and 78.6 per cent work in the United States (Freelon et al. 2023). Calls for greater 'citation justice' (Kwon 2022), 'citation diversity' (Freelon et al. 2023), and a more radical feminist politics of citation (Ahmed 2017) have multiplied of late, drawing increasing attention to underrepresented and marginalized writers, scholars, thinkers, and intellectuals. Although such interventions have been recognized as predominantly small-scale and long-term initiatives, they have served to pinpoint the overwhelming concentration of epistemological dominance and influence in academia, and in doing so they have put forward an equity-seeking agenda for the ways in which knowledge production can be reimagined.

Calls for a decentring of whiteness in the academy are intrinsically tied to the broader call to decolonize the university. Through our ongoing explorations of feminist theory, philosophy, and politics, the reading group has given shape to a form of shared feminist praxis capable of instigating the pursuit of new desire lines and lines of inquiry. My own trajectory as part of the group has been punctuated by a broader desire to participate in a re-education of sorts that has led me to question the core of my subjectivity and positionality as an academic. As Gloria Anzaldúa's work on the geography of selves reminds us, '[t]he places where I've lived have had an impact on my psyche, left a mark on every cell in my body' (2015: 68). In terms of articulating my own geography of the self, I identify as a white, cisgender male settler academic residing in K'jipuktuk, Mi'kma'ki, the unceded, unsurrendered, and ancestral territory of the Mi'kmaq people.[2] I grew up in a suburb of Sudbury, Ontario (Atikameksheng Anishnawbek land), home to one of the longest-running mining operations in the world. Surrounded by family and neighbours who worked in schools, hospitals, and mines, I always identified as belonging to a broader working-class community, but I certainly benefited from the privileges of a middle-class upbringing. The children of French-Canadian and Irish settler parents, my two older siblings and I were raised and educated in a French- and Irish-Catholic environment. The education we received in the French Catholic system did not prepare us to know anything about the legacy of colonialism in Canada, nor did it offer any opportunities to learn about Canada's role in the expansion of settler capitalism (see Shipley 2020).[3]

In many ways, the reading group has functioned as a social, intellectual, and care-oriented environment in which to grapple with the ongoing constellation of calls for broader societal reckoning. As Pavitra Sundar and Debashree Mukherjee explain in their editors' introduction to a special issue of *Feminist Media Histories* ('Decolonial Feminisms: In Media Res'), their initial call for papers (CFP) took seriously the intersecting calls to decolonize and to engage in reckoning, in what amounted to 'a call to dismantle structures of racial capitalism, carcerality, Brahminical patriarchy, ecological extraction, and the global division of gendered labor' (2022: 3). Such calls to action have precipitated a major reorientation in my thinking, research, teaching, and service: they have inspired me to reckon with my own past and present complicities in sustaining settler colonial institutions and in maintaining oppressive social and institutional status quos (Forrest et al. 2024). Following Leah Decter and Carla Taunton, I am careful to implicate myself, as a white settler academic, as a beneficiary of settler colonialism regardless of my actions, and I am attuned to the fact that the '*ongoing* colonial project positions me as dominant or what feminist sociologist and activist Sunera Thobani refers to as "exalted" subjects' (2022: 88, original emphasis).[4] Resisting the temptation to merely absolve myself of any responsibility or accountability – a default manoeuvre that Eve Tuck and Wayne K. Yang (2012) have called 'settler moves to innocence' – I have continued to stay with the trouble that is my subjectivity and status as a settler academic in Turtle Island, opting instead to work in a spirit of humility and to serve with purpose and sincerity as an ally in the broader project of decolonization. As Timothy Murphy makes clear, allyship requires sustained action, not public posturing; allyship involves 'acts of burning away some of our privilege' and it rests on the notion that 'we have to *use our privileges to end our privileges*' (2015: n.pag., original emphasis). Although the book bares a fashionable, if not trendy, title and subject matter, *Decolonial Media Imaginaries* represents a modest expression of 'decolonial solidarity' (Tuck and Yang 2012: 28) and a sincere attempt to participate in and contribute to one of many discussions animating the decolonial politics of struggle of the twenty-first century. Inspired most recently by the work of Rolando Vázquez, I see this work as a form of knowledge production rooted in the praxis of decolonial 'thinking from a shared legacy' (2020: xxv) and in the awareness of an 'infinite indebtedness to others' (2020: xxvi). Despite the severe sociopolitical, environmental, and existential challenges of the present and not-so-distant future, this book retains an optimistic outlook. By engaging the notion of imaginaries-work and by connecting the latter to the question of futurities – especially through the prism of decolonial politics – I have sought to counterbalance the oppressive weight of capitalist and colonialist dominance with the passion and clarity of what Avtar Brah has called 'decolonial imaginings' (2022). In describing the context surrounding the book's conception and subsequent completion, I have attempted to revisit a period of major social and political upheaval and to delimit the redrawing of my own scholarly orientations and commitments. This preface is not intended to pre-emptively deflect any critiques or criticism that may emerge in the wake of the book's publication, but rather to identify and articulate the motivations and broader rationale underpinning this project. My hope is that projects of this kind will contribute to the decolonial politics at play in the enactment of 'a pedagogy of reparations', in the words of Usha Iyer, 'a proliferation of demands, manifestos, and countermanifestos that become impossible to ignore' (2022a: 186).

Acknowledgements

Much in the way some of the most exciting and fulfilling work comes to materialize, this project came into being slowly, steadily, and even imperceptibly. In the fall of 2019, casual discussions with my friend and colleague, Mariana Prandini Assis, would eventually inspire us to co-organize a reading group dedicated to feminist scholar Sara Ahmed. Founded in January 2020, the reading group offered the best of what's possible when people and ideas occupy a central place in one's weekly activities. Unbeknownst to us then, the reading group would go on to function as something of a lifeline for various members, especially during the early stages of the COVID-19 pandemic. Propelled by Sara Ahmed's expansive work, the group would eventually pivot towards reading other important thinkers, writers, and scholars: Alexis Shotwell, Imani Perry, Kathi Weeks, Patricia Hill Collins, Silvia Federici, Judith Butler, Sylvia Wynter, Katherine McKittrick, la paperson, Françoise Vergès, José Medina, Gloria Anzaldúa, Robyn Maynard, Leanne Betasamosake Simpson, Adrienne Rich, Silvia Rivera Cusicanqui, El Jones, and Mikaela Luttrell-Rowland, among others. Our shared commitments to reading together over time created room for our group to engage in regular exchanges on timely issues and topics that may have escaped us had we not agreed to embark on this reading-intensive journey. Reading these challenging texts with friends, colleagues, and newcomers – in a warm, encouraging, social, and empathetic environment – created the best conditions I've ever experienced to learn about and deepen my understanding of things normally far beyond my grasp. It was during this period that I began to read more deeply about anticolonial struggles and decolonial politics. Without the support, encouragement, care, reciprocity, and constancy emanating from the group, I may have been steered towards reproducing some of the more well-trodden facets of my own research trajectory. Instead, I have been inspired to seek out and cultivate new desire lines rooted in friendship and solidarity. A note of special thanks and deep appreciation to each member of the reading group: Mariana Prandini Assis, Michelle Forrest, Columba Gonzalez, Angela Henderson, Renee Jackson, Mikaela Luttrell-Rowland, Lindsey MacCallum,

Suzanne McCullagh, Renée McKinstry, Maki Motapanyane, Ellen Shaffner, Scott Stoneman, and Sepideh Zabeti.

The seeds of this book first germinated during a yearlong research sabbatical (2021–22) facilitated by Mount Saint Vincent University (MSVU). Having cleared my desk of any lingering research projects, I decided to dedicate the entire year to reading promiscuously. With a very long, semi-structured reading list before me, I allowed for curiosity and serendipity to guide me. The combination of reading with others (reading group) and reading alone (sabbatical) cleared the way for me to imagine new possibilities for my research. The kernel of the larger idea for this book would only come well after my sabbatical had come to an end, with the announcement of a forthcoming international symposium on the theme of 'Media Imaginaries'. In March 2023, I would rehearse my first musings on the topic of decolonial media imaginaries at Lund University. Although early drafts associated with the book were presented at the Canadian Communication Association and Console-ing Passions, I am especially grateful to colleagues who attended the Marcus Wallenberg symposia in Lund (2023) and Jönköping (2024) – among them, Annette Hill, Simon Dawes, and Stuart Poyntz. Thank you for your sincere engagement with my work.

The earliest and most encouraging feedback I received would come from friends and mentors. Many thanks to Suzanne McCullagh and Tanner Mirrlees for reading the first scribbles associated with the project-as-book, and for offering generous and insightful feedback – I am forever grateful to count you among my best friends. Eternal thanks to my dear friend and mentor Mark Lipton for providing much-needed in-depth and illuminating rap sessions on how to proceed in the early stages of this project. Twenty years on, you continue to inspire me with the breadth and depth of your knowledge, compassion, ingenuity, humour, and soul. Special thanks to my editor, Julia Brockley, who has been onboard with the project since the very beginning. Thank you, Julia, for making this such a seamless and enjoyable undertaking. Your endless supply of enthusiasm and encouragement has not gone unnoticed. Many thanks to my production manager, Tian Greaves, for the care, patience, diligence, and expertise you showed throughout the entire process. I am grateful to you and the outstanding production team at Intellect for delivering an inspired and beautiful book to behold. Much appreciation and gratitude to MSVU graduate students Gaffar Oladayo Asanbe and Renée McKinstry, whose efforts ensured a frictionless transition from manuscript to polished book. I am also truly grateful to the peer reviewers of this manuscript for their generous and insightful contributions. I have never been so fortunate to receive such detailed, comprehensive, constructive, and ultimately, encouraging feedback. Your insights have not only strengthened and sharpened many aspects of the book, they have also offered me new directions for future work.

Finally, this project on how to dream and build otherwise worlds would have been unthinkable without the people with whom I dream and build for the future. To Lisa, thank you for creating room and space in our lives to dream and to fashion things that fall outside the realm of the readymade and the status quo. Aside from having introduced me to many of the examples and case studies that illuminate the core of this book's intellectual contributions, you have offered me countless moments for engaged discussion, feedback, and reflection. Of the many back-and-forth, sustained conversations we've had over the past few years concerning this ever-evolving project, I want to thank you for reminding me to travel light, to seek adventure, to keep things fresh, to invite others to collaborate, to redraw the lines of possibility – and to have fun! To Matisse, you have been the brightest light in my field of vision since the day you graced us with your presence. Life has never been nor will it ever be the same. To witness you grow and blossom in real-time with every coming day has been a most humbling and awe-inspiring experience. You add all of the best colour, texture, sound, shape, vibrancy, humour, and laughter to our everyday. You arouse in me 'the optimism of the will' to participate in and contribute to the decolonial politics afoot today so as to bring about the decolonial futures of tomorrow.

K'jipuktuk, Mi'kma'ki, the unceded, unsurrendered, and ancestral territory of the Mi'kmaq people

February 2025

NOTES

1. I'd initially reached out to Sara Ahmed via Twitter to ask what books she would recommend for our reading group, to which she suggested the following list (a list we happily adopted): *The Cultural Politics of Emotion* (2004), *Queer Phenomenology: Orientations, Objects, Others* (2006), *Living a Feminist Life* (2017), and *What's the Use: On the Uses of Use* (2019).
2. I am grateful to Max Liboiron (2021: 3) for highlighting the distinction between marked and unmarked settler scholars – an unmarked setter-scholar participates in the re-centring of settlers and whiteness as 'an unexceptional norm'.
3. This passage first appeared in Forrest et al. (2024) – an article published in a groundbreaking Special Issue of *Studies in Social Justice*, entitled 'Reckoning, repair, reworlding: The (in)humanities, artistic practices, and planetary crisis'.
4. I am equally grateful to Catherine E. Walsh for her reflections on whiteness, privilege, obligation, and responsibility: 'It is the responsibility and obligation to use my whiteness in what I understand today as opening, making, and widening cracks, all of which necessarily entails the never-ending processes of decolonizing and deschooling, including – and most especially – of myself' (2023: 84).

1

Introduction: Imaginaries-Work Through a Decolonial Lens

In July 2024, the Haida Nation and the Government of British Columbia reached a historic agreement that recognizes Haida Aboriginal title over the islands of Haida Gwaii. After decades of negotiations, over two hundred islands of Haida Gwaii (comprising approximately half a million hectares of Crown land) will be returned to the Indigenous peoples of Haida Nation as part of what has been called a 'first-of-its-kind negotiated agreement' (Pandey-Kanaan 2024). The Gaayhllxid/Gíhlagalgang 'Rising Tide' agreement establishes a process for the Haida to take over land conservation and the broader protection of the islands. According to Gaagwiis, president of the Council of the Haida Nation, the shoring up of Aboriginal title 'moves us from an adversarial position to actually [being] able to properly collaborate and co-operate with the people of the islands who've come to settle and live here' (Moran 2024). The agreement and accompanying legislation represent a watershed moment in the expression of Indigenous sovereignty and self-determination on Turtle Island (Canada). Although jurisdiction over public services such as education, health, transportation, and emergency services will continue under municipal and provincial supervision, the Haida will finally see their place as custodians and protectors of the land restored. For B.C. Premier, David Eby, the agreement will not only increase prosperity for the Haida, the Haida Gwaii community, and the province as a whole, but also model a way for other Indigenous nations to have their title recognized (Cecco 2024). Put another way, this rematriation of land sets a new precedent for how other Indigenous communities across Turtle Island might go about securing greater and greater sovereignty. Under these new arrangements, Indigenous futures are given a radically different trajectory: with communities no longer having to engage by default in adversarial, defensive, or refusal-based politics, they will be afforded greater freedom to deepen their connections to the land, history, culture, and values of their territory. Such new arrangements momentarily spark the popular imagination to conceive of nation states such as Canada and Indigenous nations such as the Haida as preparing the way for emergent forms of decolonial politics to proliferate more widely.

2024 would also mark the release of *Yintah*, 'a documentary on a decade of Wet'suwet'en resistance' (Yintah 2024). The film documents the ongoing struggles of the Indigenous peoples of Wet'suwet'en to protect their ancestral lands from both the Canadian nation state and some of the world's most powerful fossil fuel companies. The film captures the decade-long resistance efforts of the Wet'suwet'en to maintain sovereignty over their lands during a period of sustained encroachment on the part of petrochemical commercial interests. The Canadian Government's approval in 2019 of a $40-billion natural gas export infrastructure project – including a 670-km Coastal GasLink pipeline (Crawford 2018) – would prove a pivotal moment for the Wet'suwet'en, in that they would come to stand in direct opposition to the realization of this project. As Aboriginal title holders of the land, the Wet'suwet'en have maintained that the Coastal GasLink (CGL) pipeline project (as well as any other extractivist projects to have been proposed) have no place or legitimacy on their territory. The combined imposition and violence of the nation state and fossil fuel interests have led to the forced removal of Wet'suwet'en peoples (and their supporters) from their territory, and have accelerated the expropriation and theft of their land. Such efforts to dispossess Indigenous peoples constitute flagrant violations of a 1997 Supreme Court of Canada decision that reaffirmed hereditary chiefs' jurisdiction over their territory (Bellrichard and Barrera 2020). Without Wet'suwet'en consent, the CGL pipeline represents the very worst aspects of settler capitalism in Canada. As Darrin Barney has shown, pipelines are more than just devices for transporting oil: 'They are also technologies that manufacture and intensify the inequalities that are a structural characteristic of petroleum economies everywhere. This, it would seem, is who we [Canadians] are and what we do' (2017: 94). Whereas Barney suggests that Canada is a pipeline nation, Shipley goes even further in arguing that Canada is irrefutably defined by settler capitalism and the colonial imagination, two core ideological and material premises that are 'inseparable from what Canada is and does' (2020: 508). The formal announcement of the CGL project would offer a glimpse of the nation state's attempts to proliferate an ideal imaginary, one in which Canada translates the 'single largest private investment in Canadian history' as the means for developing an energy infrastructure that is accountable to the environment and Indigenous people, responsive to the challenges associated with climate change, and robust enough to create jobs and increase prosperity (Crawford 2018). As then B.C. Premier John Horgan stated during the press conference, 'British Columbians want a future that brings opportunities for them and their kids in the communities they call home, while living up to our responsibilities to guarantee clean air, land and water for the generations that follow' (cited in Crawford 2018: n.pag.). The peddling of such an imaginary is very much informed by settler capitalism and the colonial imagination – and it stands in direct contrast with the imaginaries-work inspired by the Wet'suwet'en, who present themselves as protectors and custodians of the land, and as communities who continue to fight to secure the futures of coming generations' title to the land.

The Haida Nation and Wet'suwet'en represent but two of the over six hundred and thirty Indigenous First Nations communities of Turtle Island ('First Nations'), but their struggles to survive, thrive, and achieve full sovereignty under the oppressive settler-colonial-capitalist context that is present-day Canada have endured. Whereas the Wet'suwet'en story is indicative of a much more pernicious, corrosive, and destructive presence on the part of the Canadian nation state, both the federal and provincial governments remain deliberate in their conjuring of imaginaries that invoke reciprocity and good relations, accountability and prosperity, as well as visions of a bright future. The violent removal of the Wet'suwet'en from their territory during periods of sustained non-violent protest, in addition to the ecological destruction and damage wrought via the construction of the pipeline (as depicted in *Yintah*) serve as decisive evidence that the nation state's imaginaries are not reserved for Indigenous peoples in Canada. On the other hand, the imaginaries and futures described by both the Haida and Wet'suwet'en offer visions of Indigenous self-determination wherein each respective community asserts its sovereignty in the protection and oversight of the land, as well as the autonomy to express their own distinct ways of living and being. The Haida's recent path towards sovereignty and self-determination is the result of decades of struggle against, and negotiations with, the nation state. Even in their understanding of the title agreement with the province of British Columbia, the imaginary is of a different nature. As longtime Haida activist, Guujaaw Edenshaw, has affirmed:

> [The title] doesn't come from the Crown, doesn't come from the court. It comes from our ancestry [...] The energy that has been going to fighting over the last 50 years, 100 years can turn to creating and building on our people's strength.
>
> (cited in Moran 2024: n.pag.)

Here the imaginary is firmly anchored in the past through the Haida's lineage to its ancestry and also situated in the present and future flourishing of its broader community. The imaginaries-work of the Haida, Wet'suwet'en, and the Canadian nation state serve as this book's point of departure for exploring the intersections between dominant/hegemonic imaginaries and decolonial politics.

Decolonial Media Imaginaries (*DMI*) begins from the basic premise that imaginaries serve an important role in the articulation and elaboration of identity, sociality, collectivity, and solidarity, especially in terms of the co-fashioning of ways of life and living. Imaginaries are designed to be inhabited and eventually to be lived in. The most dominant imaginaries of the industrialist past and late-capitalist present have been most finely attuned to expanding the influence of colonial, capitalist, and neo-liberal priorities and imperatives. One of the consequences associated with the circulation of these dominant imaginaries has been the marginalization and diminishment of other modes of representation that illuminate alternative ways of living that run counter to these powerful tools of worldmaking. *DMI* lays the groundwork to examine the power and limitations of both dominant and marginalized imaginaries, suggesting that the work imaginaries perform is ongoing, longstanding, and deeply embedded in broader historical, political, and geographical currents. As such, this book offers a more speculative, albeit theoretically and conceptually engaged discussion surrounding the future viability and vitality of decolonial media imaginaries as instruments for decolonial worldbuilding.

This book pivots away from the digital, technological, and sublime imaginaries created in the service of global capitalism to foreground the potential viability and generativity of cultivating decolonial media imaginaries. To do so, I situate the work of a wide variety of Indigenous, postcolonial, feminist, and critical thinkers to better illuminate the desire lines that lead to decolonial imaginaries and beyond. Among the decolonial desires articulated, scholars and activists have called for the rematriation of land, the regeneration of multispecies relations, the forwarding of Indigenous and Black futures, as well as the expansion of decolonial technologies and emancipatory designs. In foregrounding the vitality and necessity of these non-linear paths towards decolonial relations and arrangements, we come up against the sheer weight of neocolonial and capitalist forces which have become deeply engrained in the soil, air, water, and natural environments upon which all species depend. Indeed, to engage in the creation of decolonial media imaginaries is to withdraw and disinvest from the extractivist logics that pervade contemporary life and culture, and to invest in and deepen our commitments to sustainable life and just relations. *Decolonial Media Imaginaries* thus simultaneously grapples with the contradictions, counter-forces, and solidarities underpinning the struggle for decolonial futures.

Resisting the urge to merely theorize and/or dream up what a decolonial media imaginary might most closely resemble, this work also invokes the terrain prepared by decolonial scholars, settler academics, artists, and collectives to draw attention to the strategies, tools, tactics, and praxis that may be useful in bringing decolonial futures more closely within reach. Indeed, this project weaves together strands from existing scholarship to illuminate the already active and vibrant work on decolonial radical politics and infuses the latter in the largely undertheorized realm of decolonial media imaginaries. Some of the most important work to emerge of late has been firmly situated within the confines of colonial institutions (namely, places of higher learning), and this research continues to place a great deal of emphasis on subverting capitalism, delinking from Western epistemology, advancing knowledge from the Global South, and sustaining pedagogical drives towards reparations.

Decolonization and the decolonial as invitation to reckon

The book's core area of inquiry – decolonial media imaginaries – cannot be easily separated or untangled from questions pertaining to power, epistemology, ideology, infrastructure, land, labour, politics, and imagination. The book begins with an acknowledgement of the devastating legacies associated with colonialism and empire. According to the Truth and Reconciliation Commission of Canada's final report (2015: 44–45), the early European-based colonization period is best characterized as an era of military conquest, mass migration, unbridled expansion, massive land expropriation, and wealth generation – all of which constituted disastrous outcomes for Indigenous peoples the world over. Of particular note here is the degree to which colonialism as a near-totalizing system of oppression would enable European colonial powers to lay claim to most of the earth's surface, including land mass and the seas (Howe 2002: 62). According to Ashley Dawson, imperialist ideologies of domination used to 'justify European expropriation of Indigenous people and their land, also established an exploitative attitude towards flora and fauna in the colonies' (2022: 62). As Gord Hill explains in *500 Years of Indigenous Resistance*, the very foundations of colonialism saw its purest expression in the interrelated projects of 'exploiting the lands and peoples to the fullest' (2010: 15) – so much so, Hill suggests, that the period beginning in/around 1492 in the Americas is most clearly distilled through the exercise of economic expansion, land exploitation, and human extermination. In terms of the genocidal scale attributed to European colonial powers during a 100-period beginning in the sixteenth century, the populations of Indigenous peoples were decimated, declining from approximately 70–100 million to around 12 million; the Aztec nation, for example, saw its population reduced from 30 million to 3 million in a 50-year period (Hill 2010: 17). European (or Western) colonialism is thus a form of imperialism that deploys strategies of colonization in the interests of conquering populations, administering distant territories, and exploiting the local populations' resources and labour (Beaule 2017: 6).

It is during the early colonial era that the idea of modernity would begin its ascendancy as 'a discourse that promises happiness and salvation through conversion, progress, civilization, modernization, development, and market democracy' (Mignolo and Walsh 2018: 142). The onset of settler colonialism (a foundational element of both colonialism and modernity) would bring about the elaboration of an enduring structure predicated on the elimination of Indigenous peoples and on the usurpation of land; as Patrick Wolfe has argued, it created the conditions for 'settler colonizers [to] come to stay: invasion is a structure not an event' (2006: 388). Promises of wealth and class status served in part to cement settler commitments to the project of colonization, as would 'a particular realization of the imperial imagination' (Smith 2021: 26) through the proliferation of images/ imaginaries about the future nation state. Whereas colonialism represents a practice and ideology that extends globally across time and space that is centred on Western conceptions of land regimes, settler colonialism is not a historical epoch but rather 'a hegemonic bloc of time that still persists today' (Harjo 2019: 65). For Mohawk scholar Audra Simpson, 'colonialism survives in a settler form' (2014: 7) predicated on the ongoing elimination of Indigenous people, the theft of their land, and their assimilation within a white settler colonial context. Importantly, settler colonialism would have an even greater and more extensive impact – dispossessing Indigenous communities of 'futures imagined on their terms within their ways of knowing' (Harjo 2019: 10). In having painted such a dire picture, the question remains regarding how best to challenge and overturn settler colonial structures.

One of the most important conceptual tools for making light of the impacts, spectres, and hauntings associated with colonialism was introduced by Peruvian scholar Aníbal Quijano. For Quijano, the concept of coloniality or *colonialidad de poder* ('coloniality of power') was first introduced to describe a 'form of domination in the world today, once colonialism as an explicit political order was destroyed' (2007: 170). The concept of coloniality or coloniality of power has been used to describe 'a matrix of power that produces racial and gender hierarchies on the global and local levels, functioning alongside capital to maintain a modern regime of exploitation and domination' (Maldonado-Torres cited in Gongora 2022: 47). For Nelson Maldonado-Torres, coloniality not only survives colonialism, it persists as an undeniable constitutive element of modernity. The persistence and ubiquity of coloniality is upheld through a variety of ordinary everyday rituals, practices, and processes:

> It is maintained alive in books, in the criteria for academic performance, in cultural patterns, in common sense, in the self-image of peoples, in aspirations of self, and so many other aspects of our modern experience. In a way, as modern subjects we breath[e] coloniality all the time and everyday.
>
> (2007: 243)

The reverberations of coloniality are thus experienced through the organization of the social as they are expressed through our ways of learning, feeling, and knowing

(Gongora 2022: 48). It is precisely due to coloniality's ubiquitous standing that the concept of coloniality would function as a decolonial concept (Mignolo 2021b: 8). As Walter D. Mignolo and Catherine E. Walsh suggest, coloniality will likely never disappear ('coloniality is not over; it is all over' [2018: 119]), and as such, the concept of decoloniality has been advanced to signal 'calls for radical change in the dominant order and in its foundational base of capitalism, Western modernity, and ongoing colonial power' (2018: 58). As scholars of the Global South have often stated, decoloniality must be situated within the context of ongoing coloniality, and it bears repeating that the 'the political and epistemic foundations of decoloniality have been in place for over five decades' (Chiumbu and Radebe 2020: 6).

Sara Ahmed cautions us to be weary regarding the use(s) of certain words – 'the more words circulate, the less they seem to do' (2019: 149) – pointing to the limits/dangers involved in deploying a concept such as *decoloniality* and/or *decolonization*. As Eve Tuck and Wayne K. Yang argued now over a decade ago, decolonization is not a metaphor – it involves nothing less than the 'repatriation of Indigenous land and life' (2012: 21). Decolonization also refers to the 'double movement of anticolonialism and rematriation [of land]' (paperson 2017: xv, xxii). At its worst, decolonization is taken as mythology (Grosfoguel 2007: 220) or commodified and 'stripped of its connection to the vital work of Indigenous people' (Risam 2022: 137). Thus, in confronting the immensity of the actual work of decolonization, that is, in recognizing decolonization as a long-term process that involves not only the repatriation of land to Indigenous peoples but also a wholesale divestment from colonial power and colonial frameworks (Brah 2022: 11), decoloniality offers a useful option, path, analytic, and praxis for living and being otherwise (Mignolo and Walsh 2018). As Pavitra Sundar and Debashree Mukherjee insist, decoloniality represents an 'invitation to reckon with ongoing epistemic and material harms wrought through the nexus of coloniality, racial capitalism, heteropatriarchy, and the academy' (2022: 7). Reckoning here serves as an acknowledgement of these ongoing harms, as reorientation away from the colonial matrix of power, and as a move towards exploring decolonial options: 'the task is to delink from modern/colonial praxis of living and knowing, and to walk toward re-existing in the borderland and the borderlines in decolonial praxis of living, knowing, sensing, and of loving' (Mignolo and Walsh 2018: 223).

For Vanessa Machado de Oliveira, we must engage in hospicing modernity and coloniality as a means of doing away with systems built upon and maintained through 'expropriation, dispossession, destitution, genocides, and ecocides' (2021: 244). To do so involves enacting a widespread severance from modernity via disidentification, dis-ease, disenchantment, and disillusionment (2021: 214). This can also mean reckoning with, and delinking or disinvesting from modernity, a process that demands the decolonization of our unconscious. These activities are representative of the extremely difficult processes at the root of the decolonization project, undertakings that offer no incentives or rewards for doing so (2021: 239). The double bind she identifies relates to how 'decolonization is impossible when our livelihoods are underwritten by colonial violence and unsustainability' and how it is equally 'impossible to imagine decolonial futures from where we stand, having our livelihoods underwritten and unconscious mostly occupied by modernity/coloniality' (2021: 244, 181).

Su-ming Khoo and Anique Vered (2020: 233) have referred to this liminal moment as the 'invisible middle' of decoloniality, a period in which decolonial efforts can just as easily 'reflect and reproduce colonial hierarchies of power and control'. But just as the concept and practice of decoloniality can be redirected (unwittingly or not) towards colonial ends (Moyo 2020; Yates 2020), the term remains useful in grounding the problem of dehumanization under ongoing coloniality and in contextualizing the 'existence-based struggles of peoples historically subalternised by race, gender, and geopolitical struggle' (Walsh 2020: 605–06) who have endeavoured, over the last 500 years, to re-humanize and re-exist beyond the confines of colonial rule. One of the main areas of inquiry for decolonial thinkers has materialized through the question of epistemology as an exit strategy away from coloniality/modernity. As Macarena Gómez-Barris explains, 'decoloniality moves away from singularity and the reduction imposed by the European gaze toward the proliferation of epistemological possibility' (2017: 3). It is precisely the cultivation and proliferation of this epistemological possibility that animates calls for, and expressions of, decolonial politics today. Rather than positioning decoloniality as a set of practices or processes that atomize and individualize human struggles, the concept is most useful when conceived of as a shared process underpinning individual and collective action towards the transformation of structures and institutions (Mafile'o et al. 2022: 548). As Rolando Vázquez has argued, decoloniality represents the 'recovery of relationality' and an awareness that life is sustained through this 'net of relations' (2020: 155–56). In this light, decolonial politics as a form of collective expression seeks to move beyond colonial haunting in favour of cultivating 'other ways of being bound-together' (Khoo and Vered 2020: 225). The next section attends to questions of epistemic possibility and of being bound together through the proliferation of decolonial futures and imaginaries.

Imaginaries/futurities

The history of colonization in/across Turtle Island is one of unquenchable violence directed towards Indigenous peoples and the Earth. The ongoing injustices of the long colonial period into the present have foregrounded the need to bring new decolonial imaginaries into being. If, as Stuart Hall has argued, postcolonial/decolonial theoretical approaches have created room for former imperial grand narratives to be decentred and rewritten into new diasporic ones (Glück 2018: 6), the articulation of imaginaries-work may meaningfully contribute to the fashioning of alternative decolonial futures. As Vilashini Cooppan suggests in her conception of the work decolonial imaginaries could perform, the latter may illuminate

> what it means not just to live on/live after but to live *with*, with others, in solidarity, in an affinity that is not a sameness, in an aftermath consciousness that recognizes multiple, interlinked, and layered histories of dispossession, violence, and loss.
> (2019: 413, original emphasis)

At stake is a sense of being bound together in the co-creation of futures other than those of the colonial past and present, futures rooted in emancipation and liberation struggles the world over. In his recent work on radical futurisms, T. J. Demos reminds us that 'the emancipatory imagination of the not-yet must be grounded in the traditions of the oppressed' (2023b: 86) precisely because we have yet to escape the hauntings of colonial oppression.

In the face of unrelenting oppression, it is heartening to read work by Robyn Maynard and Leanne Betasamosake Simpson that insists on 'the visionary love work of worldmaking' (2022: 173) as a tool for designing decolonial imaginaries and as a driver of decolonial politics. As far as other decolonial tools are concerned, imagination and storytelling have been gaining momentum in discourses on decoloniality and decolonization (Mafile'o et al. 2022: 548) – they have even been cast as 'the raw material from which to build just futures' (Sundar and Mukherjee 2022: 3). If futurity is something that can be practiced, moulded, and given shape via community engagement in order to imagine 'unactivated possibilities' (Harjo 2019: 216), the power of imaginaries-work may hold significant promise in the realm of decolonial politics. Writing on the powerful lessons to be drawn from Afrofuturism, Jenna Hanchey points to the notion of a 'radically inclusive liberation' (2022: 285) for all (human and more-than-human species) as the foundation upon which just futures must be actualized. Nicole Furtado's research on Indigenous Futurisms explores how tapping into the power and promise of 'the imagined space of the future becomes an ideological battleground with consequences for our cultures, the planet and the next generations to come at stake' (2024: 28). Rather than follow the colonizer's scripts that envision the future as 'free from Indigenous peoples' (Kinder 2021: 71), the imaginaries-work of Indigenous Futurisms centres Indigenous peoples in depictions of the not-yet. An essential facet of imaginaries- and futurities-work is tied to the creation, circulation, and viability of sustaining decolonial visions that are decidedly for epistemic liberation/freedom and for the diversity of related struggles and lived realities (Khoo and Vered 2020: 237). Catherine E. Walsh captures this best when she speaks of a 'decolonial *for*' – a set of 'initiatives, strategies, and practices that fissure and crack colonial power' (2023: 164) – of which decolonial media imaginaries-work represents a shining example.

Book overview

Decolonial Media Imaginaries deploys a straightforward structure and organization: the book begins with an overview of both dominant/hegemonic and decolonial imaginaries, moves to a discussion of the elements and move(ment)s needed to bring decolonial futures into being, transitions towards a more sustained exploration of how artists, institutions, and media participate in the expression of decolonial politics, before offering some concluding remarks on the potential significance of media imaginaries-work for decolonial futures. Chapter 2 engages the question of imaginaries as a point of departure for exploring the work imaginaries perform in the realm of everyday life. The imaginaries we come to know hold enormous power in shaping and moulding into view the ways in which we perceive, understand, and make sense of our immediate environments and corresponding realities. Despite the impressive array of imaginaries that materialize – and have materialized – over time, space, and geography, only a small and persistent cluster of imaginaries maintain their foothold in the popular imagination. Just as various imaginaries simultaneously compete for legitimacy and acceptance, the fact remains that not all imaginaries succeed in gaining traction, winning favour, or expanding influence. To highlight the ways in which imaginaries do and do not materialize more broadly, I introduce two examples that illustrate the promise, challenges, and shortcomings of imaginaries-work – slow living and post-work – before turning to a more deeply resonant historical example: the World's Fair. The World's Fairs of the nineteenth and twentieth centuries establish a useful framework for contextualizing the defining features of imaginaries – and also for establishing a relay towards discussing media and technological imaginaries of the present. The chapter ends with an encapsulation of both the generative and problematic features associated with dominant imaginaries, highlighting the need to consider the proliferation of new imaginaries in the articulation of decolonial futures.

Just as the preceding chapter ends with a discussion concerning some of the more problematic features of dominant imaginaries, Chapter 3 begins with an exploration of how the latter imaginaries have contributed to the creation, expansion, and acceleration of destructive cycles of worldmaking. With technology and media imaginaries serving as consistent, decipherable, and ubiquitous touchstones for progress, prosperity, and human flourishing, this chapter pivots away from the digital, technological, and sublime imaginaries created in the service of global capitalism to foreground the potential viability and generativity of cultivating decolonial media imaginaries. This chapter describes the vitality and necessity of rendering visible and creating anew the desire lines that lead to decolonial futures and beyond. Because the current historical moment has been shaped by the weight of neocolonial, capitalist, and neo-liberal forces, this section of the book presents decolonial media imaginaries as a form of withdrawal and disinvestment from the extractivist logics that pervade contemporary life and culture, and as a form of investment in and commitment to sustainable life and just relations. Through two separate but related case studies, the focal point of the discussion emerges through an engagement with solar infrastructure, and Indigenous and non-Indigenous community relations. In drawing upon Indigenous-led infrastructural solarities projects in Turtle Island and the running of the salmon community revitalization efforts in Mi'kma'ki, I point to an alternative form of imaginaries-work that centres relationality, collectivity, community sovereignty, and just futures as powerful counter-forces to the more deeply entrenched and dominant media and technology imaginaries of the present.

Chapter 4 builds on the notion of alternative imaginaries-work, as expressed through the infrastructural and community-centred examples of the previous chapter, to examine another site of potentially generative decolonial possibility: the modern-day university. More specifically, this chapter emphasizes institutional critique and reform within and beyond the university as potential sites for decolonial change and transformation. The labour of academics, researchers, scholars, and arts and culture workers is foregrounded as a more elaborate case study for reflecting on the cultivation of new desire lines and the implementation of new lines of flight for challenging, subverting, or steering institutions towards decolonization efforts. This chapter situates the work of Indigenous, postcolonial, feminist, and critical media studies thinkers to put forward a more coherent picture of the contradictions, counter-forces, and solidarities that underpin the struggle for decolonial futures. This chapter revisits the terrain prepared by decolonial scholars, *scyborgs*, and settler academics to draw attention to the strategies, tools, tactics, and praxis that may be useful in bringing decolonial futures more closely with in reach.

Chapter 5 shifts away from the university as a potential site for decolonial media imaginaries-work to the contemporary art world as a representative case study for reflecting on this section's core question: Can alternatives to capitalism, occupation, and settler colonialism be conceptualized with, through, or across media, and, by extension, can media imaginaries of any kind serve the larger project of bringing decolonial futures into being? Through an exploration of

Afrofuturist and Indigenous exhibitions at The Metropolitan Museum of Art, MSVU Art Gallery, and Royal Ontario Museum, the curatorial interventions of a South Asian collective at documenta fifteen, and the Indigenous-led handover of SBC Gallery in Montreal/Tiohtià:ke, I examine the fraught and convivial ways in which artists and institutions collaborate to bring new decolonial imaginaries into being. I argue that the imaginaries-work emblematized through these examples present decolonial futures that advance Black and Indigenous sovereignty, all the while casting settler futures as undesirable and incompatible with these projects' larger visions of freedom and emancipation.

Whereas the previous chapter examines the extent to which artists and institutions participate in the elaboration of decolonial media imaginaries, Chapter 6 focuses more intently on medium-specific manifestations of decoloniality through the lens of Indigenous Futurisms. Through an exploration of video simulations, virtual reality, and a multimedia website – by way of an extended discussion of the Indigenous media art of Skawennati, Lisa Jackson, and Jennifer Wemigwans – I suggest that the lens of Indigenous futurity that animates these projects offers an essential window through which to conceive and elaborate decolonial media imaginaries. Through their respective endeavours, each artist foregrounds the representation and articulation of Indigenous futures as counterpoints to the perceived inevitability that settler colonialism will prevail, and as robust examples of Indigenous resistance and sovereignty. One important through line these art-based interventions share is a commitment to present and future Indigenous flourishing, as well as a desire to include non-Indigenous people/communities in the future elaboration of decolonial futures. This chapter ends on an optimistic note, suggesting that the creation and circulation of media imaginaries informed by Indigenous Futurisms could participate in the future popularization of decolonial politics.

The book's final chapter offers a more exploratory appraisal of the future promise and potentialities associated with decolonial media imaginaries. In framing media imaginaries-work through a decolonial lens, the book invites readers to shift their gaze away from dominant imaginaries that serve capitalism, settler colonialism, and other forms of oppressive dominance, in the interests of activating new desire lines towards decolonization. More than merely situating media imaginaries-work within the realm of media production and circulation (e.g. television, film, video games), I attempt to redraw these conceptual lines by invoking spectacle, infrastructure, community, social movements, pedagogy, praxis, and art (among other things), as fruitful areas of decolonial media inquiry. Although I remain optimistic regarding the prospect of decolonial media imaginaries in provoking wide-ranging critiques, reflections, and dialogue in relation to settler capitalism and neo-liberalism, and in pushing forward a new variety of decolonial agendas, I also acknowledge the future layers of political struggle to come. The conclusion thus points to imaginaries-work as a tool for inciting action on urgent questions tied to the politics of reckoning, incommensurability, and solidarity. Prefiguring decolonial futures is never a given in the realm of media, politics, or social movements, and as such, the groundwork must be laid for imaginaries-work to assist in cultivating deeper forms of solidarity across difference. More than this, a broader disinvestment in the project of modernity must go hand-in-hand with a deeper commitment to decolonial politics on the long road to decolonization ahead.

To conclude, the vast majority of the introduction has been reserved for establishing the context and introducing core ideas to be explored in this book. To be more specific, I have paid much closer attention to (de)coloniality and imaginaries-work as organizing frameworks, with very little attention given to media. The media component in *Decolonial Media Imaginaries* is crucial to the work presented in these pages, but I have been deliberate in de-emphasizing and even de-centring the role media has played in the social, symbolic, formal, and representational formations discussed above. Following Roger Silverstone, I situate media

> as process, as a thing doing and a thing done, and as a thing doing and a thing done at all levels, wherever human beings congregate both in real and in virtual space, where they communicate [...] where they seek in a multitude of ways, and with varying degrees of success, to connect one to the other.
>
> (1999: 4)

I draw on Silverstone, more specifically, to conceptualize media as part of the 'general texture of experience' (12) – an approach that grounds my integration of 'media' examples and case studies, ranging from media events (World's Fair), media corporations (AT&T), material infrastructure (solar panels, pipelines), social media movements (#RhodesMustFall), media curriculum, museum and gallery exhibitions, and Indigenous media art, among others. In conceiving of media along these lines, I have opted to stray from disciplinary conventions that might push me to too narrowly define decolonial media imaginaries, or sway me to only study certain kinds of media or cultural forms. In choosing to elide a certain kind of disciplinary rigour, I have aimed to produce a work that is more in dialogue with decolonial thinkers and decolonial thought, and less aligned with new and emergent currents in Communication and Media Studies. My approach has been informed by both Julietta Singh's (2017) and Lauren Fournier's (2021) calls to re-orient ourselves away from mastery, and by Natalie Loveless' (2019) invitation to engage in 'disciplinary promiscuity' or 'polydisciplinamory'. This research project began with a very basic speculative question: what role will media play in the decolonial future? A more generative and interesting question has been formulated more recently by Sasha Crawford-Holland and Lindsay LeBlanc, who ask: 'In developing a more complex understanding of media and its entanglements, how do we reconcile the increasingly colonizing force of technology with its potential as a site of decolonial creation?' (2023: 341). In what follows, I explore the intersections of (de)coloniality, media entanglements, and future-oriented imaginaries in the hopes of contributing to the growing calls to build otherwise worlds rooted in radical liberation for all.

2

Dominant Media Imaginaries: Competing Visions for Prosperous Futures

A general library search for *imaginaries* yields over 200,000 results and produces a wildly diverse array of entries. One might first note the form: audio (folk recordings), images (landscape archives), maps (literary), books (popular press), articles and theses (academic). The eye might then turn to conceptual, thematic, or disciplinary collisions: imaginaries can be spatial (place-branding in East London's digital economy), temporal (the socioeconomic and sociopolitical inequities of precarious labourers), ideological (conceptualizing race, culture, and belonging in Denmark), and carceral (exploring biopolitics and segregation through contemporary literature). The term has also been invoked to describe modernity, the nation state, geoengineering, geometry, physics, applied optics, urban planning, resource-based development, (im)migration, tourism, hybrid media activism, the global financial crisis, and so on.

I-ma-gi-na-ries is a luscious word, stretching out as far as the mouth will widen, offering both silent readers and seasoned storytellers the satisfaction of encountering so many vowels in such a compact structure. Importantly, imaginaries cannot be reduced to a simple term in search of a descriptor or superlative (i.e. social imaginaries or Africanfuturist imaginaries). Rather, the continued sway, lure, seduction, power, and force of imaginaries (*plural*) is the term's capacity to absorb interconnecting temporalities (past-present-future) and to refashion them in a variety of contexts that highlight the dynamic, multifaceted, and competing visions and desires that animate a given group, public, community, or society. For Charles Taylor, imaginaries refer to 'the way ordinary people "imagine" their social surroundings [...] [as] carried in images, stories, and legends' (2004: 23). This capacity to imaginatively conjure up or give shape to our social surroundings via images and narratives opens up important pathways for social cohesion. Building on Taylor's conceptualization of the work imaginaries perform, Dilip Gaonkar writes that imaginaries give us 'a sense of who we are, how we fit together, how we got where we are, and what we might expect from each other in carrying out collective practices that are constitutive of our way of life' (2002: 10). For Taylor and Gaonkar, then, imaginaries serve a potentially vital function in the elaboration of identity, sociality, collectivity, and solidarity, especially in terms of the co-fashioning of ways of life and living.

Imaginaries can be propagated by nation states, corporations, social movements, small collectives, professional societies, and single individuals for the purposes of shoring up power and encoding visions of 'how life ought, or ought not, to be lived' (Jasanoff 2015: 4). Thus, imaginaries are designed not only to be inhabited, but also to be eventually fully lived in. There is a slow and uneven accrual in the frequency and weight of their influence. With so many competing imaginaries vying for attention at any given moment, the (s)low hum of percolating ideas is at once difficult to grasp and near-impossible to behold. What is clear is that the imaginaries we (come to) know hold enormous power in shaping and moulding into view the ways in which we perceive, understand, and make sense of our immediate environments and corresponding realities. And the imaginaries that do *land* (there is a sense that imaginaries begin in the air, producing spellbinding vistas and panoramic delights) begin to take root and to occupy greater space in private and public manifestations of visual culture and everyday discourse. On one level, imaginaries participate in creating 'the popular vocabulary that we use to describe what we see when we see the future' (Lewis 2016: 37); on another level, symbolic landscapes or imaginaries have the capacity to structure action, 'making some kinds of actions more probable than others' (Bolin 2019: 28). Indeed, imaginaries-work has much to teach us about the ways in which language and 'performed visions of desirable futures' (Jasanoff 2015: 4) come to structure our ways of envisioning progress or the good life.

Slow living

The past decade alone has produced an impressive array of dystopian- and utopian-tinged imaginaries that have sought to win over the minds and hearts of people the world over: cryptocurrency, smart cities, autonomous robots, 3D printing, hologram entertainment, pluriversal living, space travel, and end-of-the-world apocalypse, to name but a few. Two imaginaries that have captivated my interest and curiosity relate to slowness and agency. Slow living and post-work movements, for example, have presented comprehensive and convincing visions for a different kind of prosperity and flourishing (one that runs in tandem with, but also counter to, the whims and drives of twenty-first-century capitalism). The slow movements – of which, slow food, slow media, and slow scholarship have taken pride of place in my own thinking – have generated renewed interest in the more general idea of slowing down. In a contemporary culture awash in the always-on vibrancy of speed and acceleration, slow movements have sought to cultivate slowness as not only a counterpoint to the speed(iness) of everyday life, but also as a reorientation towards slowness as an ideal. Although a binary logic can readily insert itself in the readymade juxtapositions of, say, slow food and fast food, the terrain advanced by slowness advocates has created more leeway to observe societies of speed, reflect on the mechanisms that propel acceleration systems forward, and design alternative forms of praxis to change the rhythms and pulses animating our activities. It is not that the slow must eclipse the fast, nor that the fast must always connote negative and/or destructive characteristics. 'The Slow Media manifesto' highlights this distinction in a noteworthy comparison with slow food: 'Like "Slow Food", Slow Media are not about fast consumption but about choosing the ingredients mindfully and preparing them in a concentrated manner' (Köhler et al. 2010: n.pag.). The manifesto underscores the necessity of nourishing cultures of sustainability, pleasure, quality, craft, aura, autonomy, authenticity, and mindfulness across the media spectrum. It is not merely a matter of slowing down, but a question of attunement to desirable realms of experience that are sidelined, diminished, or abandoned in cultures of speed and acceleration. The joy of creating a musical instrument, the novelty of sending or receiving handwritten letters, the pleasure of listening to albums on vinyl (preferably with other people) – these activities serve as counterpoints to other, more digitally centred ones (software use, e-mail exchanges, music streaming), and yet they need not replace any competing spheres of activity. In my reading of these movements' imaginaries, the slow is foregrounded and privileged to a degree in the interests of promoting greater reflection on our quotidian practices and how we might go about making better, more careful, more deliberate, and more life-enhancing choices about how we spend our time. The championing of the slow can be counterbalanced by the inclusion of a variety of different temporal, spatial, political, and economic considerations. Put another way, slowness and speed, including all of the granular points and degrees of acceleration and deceleration, can readily co-exist in the daily balance of things. An important lesson to be gleaned from slow movements is that, however powerful the imaginary of slowing down may be, and however desirable slowness may be as a set of values and principles, slowing down remains a realm of privilege few can truly access or enjoy. For Jennifer Rauch (2018: 31), slow media as a movement, thus, represents a timely intervention regarding the politicization of time and for introducing frameworks for imagining and accessing alternative modes of living. But as Sarah Sharma astutely reminds us, few people are economically and/or culturally privileged enough to cultivate slowness in everyday life: 'Slow living is mandated as correct yet reserved only for those who have time to make time' (2014: 134, 128). As far as imaginaries-work is concerned, the process of slowing down is essential in that it creates space to pause and reflect on the present, and on our collective sense of agency in shaping desirable futures (Farman 2018).

Researchers in the realm of slow scholarship have argued for greater slowness as a means to engage in the work of defamiliarization and demystification of labour, a process through which we may begin 'to ask questions *differently*', as well as 'to care and to care *differently*' (Loveless 2019: 107, original emphasis). Notions of defamiliarization and demystification have much to teach us about the often-exploitative arrangements that define contemporary labour and work, and they also offer an essential lens through which to grapple with/against the hegemony of dominant, mainstream, well-worn, and commonsensical ways of doing and living. For Natalie Loveless, the work of the arts (and of research-creation, more specifically) is to encourage

> modes of sensuous, aesthetic attunement, and work as a conduit to focus attention, elicit public discourse, and shape cultural imaginaries. 'How might the world be organized differently?' is a question that matters urgently, and it is a question that art – particularly art attuned to human and more-than-human social justice – asks in generative and complex ways.
>
> (2019: 16)

One important vehicle for bringing these imaginaries into being is the experience of deep thought, creativity, and problem-solving – what Maggie Berg and Barbara Seeber refer to as 'timeless time' (2016: 26). For the latter authors of *The Slow Professor*, we need to 'protect a time and a place for timeless time' because it is through these experiences that we cultivate creativity and critical thought (2016: 28), cornerstones of broader individual and collective well-being. Returning to Sharma's (2014) work on slow living, the very real constraints and barriers to producing these generative arrangements are many, and the world is not *yet* structured or organized to advance slowness as a dominant imaginary, however powerful its promise and potentialities.

Post-work

Which allows to me to pivot nicely to my second example of interest: post-work imaginaries. In *Inventing the Future*, Nick Srnicek and Alex Williams (2016) argue that the larger seductive idea in the realm of contemporary work/labour is the refusal of work and the demand for full *un*employment. The imaginary they invoke privileges 'building a post-work society on the basis of fully automating the economy, reducing the working week, implementing a universal basic income, and achieving a cultural shift in the understanding of work' (2016: 108). At the heart of this imaginary is the will to move beyond the gridlock between the winners and losers of the global labour economy. As Peter Frase puts it, 'will new technologies of production lead to greater free time for all, or will we remain locked into a cycle in which productivity gains only benefit the few, while the rest of us work longer than ever?' (2016: 18). At the very core of the idea of post-work imaginaries is the desire to cultivate individual autonomy and collective flourishing. In imagining a world beyond what Marx (2008) referred to as the 'realm of necessity' of work ('The Trinity Formula') and replacing it with what Kate Soper (2020: 180) calls 'post-growth living', we might refashion the everyday through mixed modes of making and doing (e.g. craft/artisanal work, cooperative ownership structures, greening technologies) that increase worker satisfaction and autonomy and serve to break down gender divisions of labour and income inequalities. Such visions imagine relations that resist dominance, submission, command, and obedience, and prepare the way for a world of many hierarchies of status that are no longer aligned with capital and money as the driving forces behind the former (Weeks 2011: 21; Frase 2016: 68). With the move to build post-work futures comes the elaboration of companion imaginaries that prepare the way for the material conditions associated with the desired imaginary. Universal basic income (UBI), for example, has served as an interlocking mechanism for bringing about some of the individual and collective flourishing described above. For David Graeber, UBI represents establishing 'the right of material existence for all people' (2018: 196) – a lever that would offer more people greater autonomy over how they spend their time. With these supports firmly in place, people could refuse exploitative and prescriptive forms of labour and work more along the lines imagined by Marx and Engels in *The German Ideology*,

> where nobody has one exclusive sphere of activity but each can become accomplished in any branch he [sic] wishes, society regulates the general production and thus makes it possible for me to do one thing today and another tomorrow, to hunt in the morning, fish in the afternoon, rear cattle in the evening, criticise after dinner, just as I have a mind, without ever becoming hunter, fisherman, herdsman or critic.
>
> (1970: 53)

We may or may not feel inclined to update the kinds of work/ers Marx and Engels describe for more contemporary and future-imagined kinds of labour/ers, but the overall sense of autonomy, freedom, and variety they advocated for are as powerful and desirable as ever.

As Kathi Weeks eloquently puts it, to achieve the good life of post-work imaginaries is to fully articulate a demand

> for more time not only to inhabit the spaces where we now find a life outside of waged work, but also to create spaces in which to constitute new subjectivities, new work and nonwork ethics, and new practices of care and sociality.
>
> (2011: 174)

In Weeks' view, the stakes are high; these demands are as much about 'getting a life' as they are about putting social reproduction and life atop the marquee – not a so-called life of labour and work in the service of capitalism (2011: 230–31). If post-work imaginaries are to have any sway for the future, they will have to convince human beings in affluent societies that radically different forms of collective life and individual consumption are not only possible but essential to ensuring ecological sustainability and human well-being (Soper 2020: 13). To embrace post-work imaginaries is, I would argue, to participate in a much broader project of putting care at the very centre of life (Chatzidakis et al. 2020: 5–6). The communities most affected by the global pandemic that began in 2020 – those overlooked, disregarded, and abandoned by the state – have been, out of sheer necessity, 'experimenting wildly with forms of collective care at an entirely new scale and new scope' (Maynard and Simpson 2022: 72). Unfortunately, in the absence of a post-work imaginary that delivers on the promise of greater autonomy, freedom, and ultimately, security, communities most impacted by the very harsh conditions of the present will have to devise their own collective forms of delivering care. The challenge lies in creating imaginaries capable of capturing the popular imagination and inciting action in the service of bringing these visions to fruition.

Dominant and resistant imaginaries

Having described two examples of contemporary imaginaries that have remained peripheral all the while continuing to make inroads as viable trajectories for human flourishing, I now turn to a broader discussion regarding imaginaries-work that is vital to the foundation of this book – dominant imaginaries. The above discussion on slow living and post-work has served to better situate the promise, potentialities, and challenges of bringing imaginaries-work fully into being. Indeed, the next example will attempt to shed light on the degrees to which imaginaries can be successful in materializing into more expansive visions for the present and future. In what follows, I centre the discussion by invoking the World's Fair as a site through which dominant visions of the present and future have consistently prevailed.

Fantasies, spectacles, and imaginaries

Much has been written on the World's Fair (Great Exhibition/Exposition universelle/World Expo) since its inauguration by the British in the mid-nineteenth century. Since its inception, the World's Fair has channelled a 'phantasmagoric logic' wherein buildings, technologies, machines, foodstuffs, art, architecture, and artefacts have historically served to present 'contradictory messages, ideals, and ideologies' (Kenneally and Sloan 2010: 3, 6). What these world exhibitions have consistently shared in common, Tony Bennett writes, is the desire to 'highlight the ideological economy of their organizing principles, transforming displays of machinery and industrial processes, of finished products and *objets d'art*, into material signifiers of progress – but of progress as a collective national achievement with capital as the great co-ordinator' (1988: 80). As Bennett argues, the exhibitions of the nineteenth century came to function as 'promissory notes' that would eventually deliver on utopian visions for improved social organization and urban living (1988: 95), while the World's Fairs of the twentieth tended to be fuelled by rhetorics of progress that could be 'translated into a Utopian statement about the future' (Rydell 1984: 4). In more recent twenty-first-century incarnations of the fair, the World Expo has tailored its approach more in terms of *scripting* or *formatting* imaginaries of desirable futures via 'specific articulations of desired elements such as economic growth, sustainability, and a better city life' (Hult 2013: 79), with the added emphasis on justifying and deepening investments in science, technology, and innovation.

Jeffrey Auerbach's (1999) study of the Great Exhibition of 1851 (i.e. the Crystal Palace Exhibition) offers an important lens through which to appreciate the defining tensions at work in these expansive events. Whereas the Great Exhibition has long stood as a leading symbol for the peace, progress, and prosperity of the mid-Victorian era, Auerbach argues that it more closely symbolizes 'fierce nationalistic competition and xenophobia in international affairs; the persistence of aristocratic power; the increasing division of British society into classes; the beginnings of British economic declines; and, the entrenchment of racial attitudes that would characterize the expanding British empire' (1999: 107–08). World exhibitions are protean in nature, expansive in their execution, and far-reaching in their aspirations. The discrepancies between the vaunted imaginaries put forward and the less-than-representative corresponding realities of the moment or era have something to teach us about the enduring power imaginaries hold over the popular imagination and public memory. 'Representations of imperial, national, and colonial identities, power, and production' have been common in world exhibitions since their inception (Hoffenberg 2001: 20). At their very worst, exhibitions of the nineteenth and early twentieth centuries would feature 'human showcases' comprising racist displays that brought together colonized peoples (predominantly African and Asian) with the intention of encouraging visitors to regard the latter as 'a lower form of life'; for Paul Greenhalgh (1988: 109), the damage of these dehumanizing practices remains unrepaired. In a very sober reading of the ethnological villages featured in America's turn-of-the-century fairs (e.g. Philippines Reservation), Robert Rydell notes that white visitors were invited to see non-whites on display as 'natural resources to be exploited as readily as mineral deposits' (1993: 20–21), a mechanism that would encourage white Americans to affirm their own cultural and racial superiority. According to Rolando Vázquez, such colonial exhibitions constituted 'training grounds for the imperial gaze' (2020: 41) that celebrated whiteness through the spectacularization and racialization of the other. In sum, these exhibitions are best described as events that wove together contradictory values – positive notions of progress underwritten by organized forms of exploitation, oppression, and dehumanization (Greenhalgh 1988: 79). Although the fairs aspired to be taken seriously as opportunities for civic education and social planning (Kenneally and Sloan 2010: 9), it was impossible to witness a world event of this kind as anything other than a site consistently marked by international competition, 'military technology, imperial conquest and abject racism' (Greenhalgh 1988: 17).

Closely aligned with these machinations has been a much more pronounced project of first presenting then seeking to implement ideas about the future that simultaneously prioritize and serve the interests of the ruling classes and world leaders (Shulruff and Wyman 2023: 3). As Astrid Nordin roundly puts it, '[w]orld fairs were from the outset an exercise where self/other relations were heavily tinted by imperialism' (2012: 245), an exercise that fuelled competition and fostered ongoing practices of a kind of one-upmanship between imperial nations such as Great Britain and France (Levin 2021: 1217). Maurice Roche (2000) has quite rightly characterized exhibitions of this kind (including the Olympic Games) as *mega-events* that express power and influence through capitalist, nationalist, and imperialist flows and logics. Within the American context, these century-of-progress expositions helped cohere both elite and middle-class interests around a blueprint for the future that characterized progress 'as synonymous with material growth, scientific and technological advance, and a continued acceptance of "empire as a way of life"' (Rydell 1993: 214–15). As Miriam Levin (2021: 1215) recounts, European World's Fairs emphasized economic development and infrastructural expansion, whereas their American counterparts foregrounded the creation of knowledge-producing institutions such as museums and universities. Wrapped up within the larger discourses of imperialist and capitalist logics put firmly on display through these exhibitions is the notion that World's Fair visitors and observers are invited down the path that requires 'we see ourselves as in need of incessant self-modernization if we're to get to where we're headed' (Bennett 1991: 35) – a world defined by unrelenting progress.

The power of imaginaries lies in their ability to attend to, arouse, and capture attention in both short-term and long-term configurations. World's Fair exhibitions have been particularly effective in producing imaginaries capable of fascinating and titillating visitors; as Penelope Harvey describes in her anthropological takeaway from Expo '92 in Seville, the exhibition 'fascinated visitors by its displays of effects, producing contexts and constructs for visitors to consume, both as representation and as the vehicles for straight sensation' (1996: 175). Not to reduce the elaboration of imaginaries to the interlocking realms of consumption and sensation, but the latter do perform the work of viscerally interpellating visitors into imagined spaces and locations. Somewhere in the balance between sensation and consumption lies all the ambivalence and ambiguity these events generate, especially for exhibition visitors. As Harvey illustrates in her account of the Seville Expo (the last universal exhibition of the century[1]), an average couple visiting from the Andalusian countryside would have navigated the site to witness the

> expression of desires for consumer goods, or for the acquisition of experience which can be displayed and traded in conversations or in the form of material souvenirs, sites in which to seek shelter from the heat, places to rest weary feet, opportunities to avoid the queues.
>
> (1996: 2)

Aside from serendipitously and/or strategically mapping their activities for the day, Harvey's visitors might also leave room to deliberate on the intentions underpinning certain exhibitions, to collect or exchange handouts, to compare notes with other visitors on their experiences of certain pavilions, to discuss the intertextual references and reflexive ironies to be found in the architecture and exhibition displays, to take pictures and to send postcards that capture certain features or aspects that piqued one's interest (1996: 2). The larger point that Harvey makes is that the process of *seeing the world as exhibition* constitutes as a core imaginary that is so much a part of the experience of visiting these events that they become normalized, dominant, and self-evident. As Harvey asserts, visitors may have identified some discontinuities, inconsistencies, or disappointments, '[b]ut I doubt that they returned home thinking how strange it was to see the world as exhibition' (1996: 3). The ramifications associated with this kind of imaginaries-work are neatly distilled by Vázquez who argues that these exhibitions so effectively shore up the aesthetic order of modernity/coloniality that 'what is produced as artifice becomes the reality of experience' (2020: xxi).

The World's Fair has consistently reinforced the notion that spectacles, fantasies, and imaginaries should serve as the default touchstones upon which visions of the future are elaborated. The fax machine (1851), telephone (1876), Ferris wheel

(1893), dishwasher (1893), X-ray machine (1904), video calling machine (1964), jetpack (1964), and touch screen (1982) all debuted in World's Fairs, solidifying the central place of imaginary-building through emerging technology (Findling and Pelle 1990; Olito 2019; Nguyen 2016). One spectacularly effective example of the ossification of a technological vision of the future materialized in the years following General Motors' Futurama exhibit (1939–40), foretelling 'the car-centric urban visions' of the twentieth century (Mattern 2020: 135). These inventions and innovations may not have all gained widespread success or notoriety, but they did pave the way for stirring the popular imagination of visitors, onlookers, commenters, historians, critics, and society at large to anticipate future advances in the realm of science, technology, manufacturing, architecture, administration, logistics, and representation, and to look to the not-so-distant future as a place of progress and prosperity. Indeed, as Rydell recounts, World's Fairs of the twentieth century were branded century-of-progress expositions, and in instances such as the Golden Gate International Exposition of 1939, the fantasy of progress was presented as paradise regained through industry, adventure, and leisure 'bound together in a romance of empire' (1993: 130). Such characterizations do not appear to be anomalous within the context of the World's Fair histories.

The swell of fantasy coupled with visions of prosperous futures is a defining feature of dominant media imaginaries. Vincent Mosco's work on the digital sublime captures the essence of how such imaginaries continue to engrain themselves in everyday life:

> Put simply, we want to believe that our era is unique in transforming the world as we have known it. The end is preferred to more of the same; the transcendent to the routine; the sublime to the banal. So we not only view our age as revolutionary. We forget that others looked at earlier technologies in much the same way.
>
> (2004: 118)

Mosco's study of the telegraph, electricity, telephone, radio, television, and the internet highlights the degree to which history is endlessly punctuated by myth-making about technology, to such an extent that the processes through which shared myths about new media and technology are created give rise to 'widespread historical amnesia' (2004: 117). The pronouncements, visions, and rhetorics surrounding so-called utopian technologies leave us ensnared by the promise of more leisure, less toil, improved quality of life, greater freedom, more pleasure, increased satisfaction, unparalleled harmony, and so on. Media imaginaries are simultaneously a byproduct of, and reinforced by, the power of myth. For Roland Barthes, myth is best conceived of as a 'conjuring trick' that turns 'reality inside out' in the interests of rendering things pure, innocent, and natural – and of producing eternal justifications for the appearance of things as 'statements of fact' (1957: 142). To summarize briefly: the sway of the dominant utopian imaginary is achieved through a collectively produced widespread historical amnesia that creates space for new mythmaking technology and media apparatuses to assume an innocent, natural, and commonsensical place in our everyday lives. Add to this the notion that media imaginaries are all-too-often steeped in projections of binary logic or thinking: utopia/dystopia, hope/despair, optimism/pessimism, positive/negative – with technology and media placed either at the 'centre of an ailing society or a flourishing community' (Lim 2018: 375). The power these imaginaries hold can be most closely tied to the creation, circulation, and bolstering of fantasies within the realm of media and technology history. As Simone Natale and Gabriele Balbi have argued,

> Fantasies are produced by the agency of different social groups, and they in turn lead to the development of different ideas of media. Studying these fantasies means analyzing the cultural grounds and the cultural possibilities through which media have been built, changed, saved, and also 'killed' or forgotten. In sum, the study of media fantasies touches on the grounds in which media history can be rooted: the life, change, and perception of media technologies.
>
> (2014: 212)

For transdisciplinary media scholar Shannon Mattern (2020: 139), fantasy and spectacle are infused within even the most painfully banal areas of modern life (e.g. analogue record-keeping), only with enough power and efficacy that the latter have been successful in powering fantasies of, for example, efficient modern offices, and by extension, efficient modern cities. So powerful are the driving forces underpinning the media imaginaries behind artificial intelligence (AI), to use a more timely example, that not only has the aura of AI's future inevitability bypassed most of the critical societal checkpoints, its ascending star in the popular imagination has led to a 'radical redrawing of civic life, where centers of power are strengthened by tools that see with the logics of capital, policing, and militarization' (Crawford 2021: 223). And with this redrawing of the contours of civic life we have been seduced and/or distracted by the hollowness of these imaginaries' projects. On the one hand, it has become all-too-easy to embrace the premise that technologies can and will 'spontaneously produce the conditions of equity, justice or freedom' (Greenfield 2017: 302); on the other hand, as Mullaney et al. have argued, it has become 'ever more urgent to recognize that technological progress without social accountability is not real progress' (2020: 20). In many ways, the promissory notes associated with progress that would come to define the World's Fairs of yesterday have continued to resonate loudly, with the selling point remaining within the realm of science and technology. As Tom McDonough suggests, our ever-increasing drives spurred by the Promethean quest for progress have only further exacerbated the 'uncritical acceptance of technological progress' (2010: 91). The dominant imaginaries of our time have contributed greatly to the consolidation and proliferation of very narrowly defined views of technology and media within a predominantly global capitalist framework. The next chapter works with and against these machinations to consider the role technology and media could play in the context of decolonial futures.

NOTE

1. Spain would spend billions towards 500th anniversary celebrations for 'Discovery of the Americas', some of which were used in conjunction with Expo '92 in Seville (Hill 2010: 6). In Chapters 5 and 6, I explore some of the contested politics at work in the elaboration of the 'Canada 150' celebrations of 2017.

3

Decolonial Media Imaginaries: Good and Right Relations, Just Futures, Community Sovereignty

In the previous chapter, I set out to describe and contextualize both marginal and dominant forms of imaginaries-work, beginning with a discussion of slow living and post-work, before turning to the World's Fair as a rich case study for exploring the ongoing vibrancy and staying power of longstanding dominant imaginaries. In this chapter, I pivot away from the World's Fair as a site through which dominant visions of the present and future have consistently prevailed towards thinking about the power and promise of decolonial imaginaries. By decolonial imaginaries, I refer to the kinds of relations, modes of being, sites of collaboration, and collective orientations precipitated by visions of the future, that propel communities towards a reckoning with the legacies of colonialism, and towards the creation of more just and equitable worlds. Although the title of this book makes reference to *decolonial* media imaginaries, it is imperative to begin this longer discussion by situating the work of media and technology imaginaries, especially given the fact that these imaginaries have long served the interests of both dominant institutions and the ruling classes. Far from contributing to the emancipatory projects associated with decolonization or decolonial politics, twenty-first-century technology and media often participate in the reproduction of settler-colonial, capitalist, and neo-liberal logics for the express purposes of furthering the aims, objectives, and goals of these elites (Benjamin 2019; Couldry and Mejias 2019; Crawford 2021; Madianou 2025). In what follows, I contrast the imaginaries espoused by the likes of former behemoth media corporation AT&T with some of the current deficiencies of modern-day internet platforms, with the goal being to highlight the discrepancies between the imaginaries produced by dominant media firms and their actual implementation or materialization. In pointing to these trappings and deficiencies, I suggest that we have reached a veritable impasse in terms of what passes as mainstream and dominant media, a stalemate of sorts that may very well precipitate a change to the structure, organization, and elaboration of our contemporary global media systems. By drawing on the internet as a potential site of intervention, I present the idea of a decolonized internet as a case study for thinking about what changes, tools, practices, and policies are needed to bring about such a seismic transformation to the world's global communication infrastructure. A radical shift of this kind would entail, among many other things, the democratization of ownership, production, and dissemination of knowledge, and a much broader struggle over access to and the elaboration of internet architectures and infrastructures (Philip 2021). Because each piece associated with decolonizing the internet requires imaginaries-work of its own, the core of this chapter involves an exploration of two case studies that present a decolonial ethos – an ongoing set of Indigenous-led solar infrastructure projects in Canada, and a community salmon project shared by Indigenous and non-Indigenous peoples in Mi'kma'ki. Together these examples illustrate the challenges, limitations, affordances, and possibilities that decolonial initiatives confront through the creation of imaginaries and in the realization of lived, embodied, and material projects.

Technopoly imaginaries

As far as media and technological imaginaries are concerned, a wide array of actors have stood to benefit from the proliferation and reification of these visions of, and desires for, the future. Among them, visionaries promising utopian living arrangements, news media engaging in the circulation of attention-grabbing stories, politicians seeking to be more closely aligned with all things technology and innovation, capitalist enterprise looking to secure new markets and expand their reach, and everyday citizen-consumers eager to increase their leisure and pleasure (Mosco 2004). Indeed, some of the leading proponents that drive these visions forward are the dominant institutions of our era; namely, governments and corporations. The peddling of these imaginaries can be deceptively simple and wholly provocative. Take, for example, a 1993 advertising campaign by AT&T, once one of the most powerful media corporations in the world. In a series of television advertisements (cajolingly entitled, *You Will*), the company forecasts a number of scenarios from everyday life in which technology fulfils the most basic, albeit unimaginable, tasks: 'Have you ever paid a toll without slowing down? Bought concert tickets from a cash machine? Or, tucked your baby in from a phone both? You will' (AT&T 1993). Here, voiceover narration is used to accompany the viewer through a series of rhetorical questions and provocative images. During a 30-second spot, the viewer witnesses a motorist paying a toll booth by scanning a credit card while driving, concertgoers purchasing tickets using a touch screen, and a mother videoconferencing with a newborn via a telephone booth. A number of these ads were created specifically for the campaign, and along with them, new visions would emerge for voice-activated door entrances, card-scannable digital medical records, synchronous audio-visual work meetings, and on-demand virtual education- and entertainment-based platforms. The attendant logic of the ads was that these advancements in technology and infrastructure were not *yet* readily available or accessible to the vast majority of everyday consumers, but that they were in the process of being realized, and that AT&T would be responsible for ushering in these welcome new changes. Nonetheless, television spots of this kind – serial in nature and redundant in its messaging – accrue a kind of generative potential that can momentarily capture one's attention and imagination to foreground the juxtaposition of improbable scenarios (e.g. using one's voice to open a door; borrowing a digital copy of a book from far away). Such speculative improbabilities are framed in a positive light, illustrating the ways in which technology is at once assistive, liberatory, and life-affirming, all the while fashioning new desire lines for technology use in everyday life. As AT&T would have it, these are imaginaries to dream about, wish for, and ultimately inhabit.

In a predictable turn, AT&T would revisit its *You Will* imaginaries 25 years after the fact (2018), so as to confirm that their visions had been realized (unironically by a host of other research labs and companies). Perhaps highlighting one key aspect of dominant imaginaries-building, the company would publish '25 years ago, AT&T predicted the future we're living now' as bona fide partner content (read: paid advertorial content) via *Wired*, one of the foremost publications on technology and innovation. To celebrate the 25th anniversary of this advertising campaign (on the *Wired* website), the company brought together experts, futurists, and philosophers 'to share their visions of what the future will be 25 years from now' (Stevenson 2018). Among their predictions are zero-waste cities powered by artificial intelligence, self-driving car networks, mixed-reality education experiences, and empathetic digital caretakers.

The fact that the imaginaries from 1993 have all since come to fruition is the least interesting aspect of this area of discussion. Of interest here are all of the human, technological, infrastructural, and ecological assemblages that were harnessed to render these visions concrete. Indeed, the concretization of these ideas into matter has come at the expense of the world's already fragile ecosystems, biospheres, and natural environments. Although the idea of measuring the ecological footprint of 'virtually' attending a business meeting from the beach (one of AT&T's imaginaries-activities) might seem beside the point, the interconnections among virtual beach meetings to networked gaming to online streaming are clear in that they represent intense natural resource-depleting activities that cannot be relegated to more neutral systems of representation that situate human practices as unproblematic or apolitical (e.g. Crawford and Joler 2019; Hogan 2018). Nor should the more colossal resource-extracting activities of, for example, global mining companies, microelectronics industries, and technology assembly contractors, be sidelined from the discussion; rather, the tireless and irreparable harms the latter have accelerated can be seen as two sides of the same coin in that both the imaginaries and the extractivist dimensions of each project are mutually operationalized. As Kate Crawford and Vladan Joler (2019) have shown, these extractive practices draw from natural resources that have taken billions of years to materialize, only to produce discardable 'devices that are often designed to be used for no more than a few years'. In yet another move designed according to a dominant imaginaries playbook, even future predictions for 2043 elide any reference to environmental strain or ecological disaster; all we know is that AI will power zero-waste cities, to which I would ask, what will these cities' neighbouring rural environs resemble? The overriding point of the imaginaries-work presented by AT&T (past-present-future) is to secure the trust and goodwill of citizen-consumers who will (in/directly) support their future endeavours. So long as the imaginaries are captivating, inspiring, and hopeful, the future costs associated with these projects can be wilfully sidelined or made irrelevant.

In terms of situating the current discussion firmly in the present moment, one recent manifestation of a dominant imaginary has emerged in the realm of cloud computing infrastructure, in what has been most commonly referred to as the cloud or big data. One of the most successful tricks proponents of the cloud and big data imaginaries have realized is the notion that digital life (broadly conceived) is ethereal, porous, intangible, and immaterial, convincing media and technology users and software adopters that digital resources leave (little to) no footprint. The broad proliferation of these narratives and their accompanying visual rhetorics have tactfully contributed to the creation and bolstering of 'a capitalist-colonialist fantasy that sustains the myth of perpetual economic growth without material limitations' (Taffel 2023: 981). As Sy Taffel (2023) has shown, the phrase 'data is the new oil' – used to connote that data has replaced oil as the world's most valuable resource – carries with it not only metaphorical and ideological connotations, but with it a whole series of assemblages tied to intensive industrial extractive processes the world over. The exploitation of human and ecological ecosystems is tucked neatly out of view, and all that is left is the apparent frictionless wonder that are the digital dataworlds of the current moment. Taffel (2023: 984) argues that oil and data, in their respective ways, have contributed greatly to geopolitical extractions of geological and economic wealth, in what has constituted an ongoing set of practices predicated on relations of ecological harm and economic inequality. Returning to Roland Barthes' (1957) formulation of myth as a conjuring trick, it is unsurprising that the commonplace discourses surrounding data as clean, natural, and immaterial have continued largely unabated into the 2020s. 'Far from being smart, green and weightless, the cloud turns out to be more akin to a miasma of toxic smog' (Taffel 2023: 987). For Sheena Wilson (2018), dominant forms of imaginaries-work are intrinsically flawed in that they pose as innovative while repackaging and reperpetuating articulations of the status quo; Wilson reminds us via Fredric Jameson that imaginaries presented as narratives of the future do more to 'demonstrate and to dramatize our incapacity to imagine the future' (cited in Wilson 2018: 385) than they do to articulate new imaginaries. The cloud, big data, and the internet all figure prominently in the proliferation of hollow and hollow-ed out imaginaries of any value (Mosco 2014).

The internet of 2024 (the current time of writing) pales in comparison to the internet imagined by the earliest champions of the World Wide Web. The early promise of a World Wide Web capable of democratizing access to information, resources, community, and self-expression, among other things, has been severely undermined by the deregulation and hypercommercialization of the internet. Cultural critic and novelist Cory Doctorow sardonically describes this ultimate downward spiral as *enshittification*. As Doctorow sees it, capitalism has eroded and destroyed virtually all that was good about the internet and digital platforms, in a process best explained via what he calls the enshittification cycle:

> Surpluses are first directed to users; then, once they're locked in, surpluses go to suppliers; then once they're locked in, the surplus is handed to shareholders and the platform becomes a useless pile of shit. From mobile app stores to Steam, from Facebook to Twitter, this is the enshittification cycle.
>
> (2023: n.pag.)

The general idea is that platform users are first enticed to join and participate on a given platform, only to be later brokered off to prospective marketers and advertisers, the latter of whom are later cornered into less-than-desirable economic arrangements, only to find that shareholders are eventually the only ones left with anything to celebrate. During this cycle, the platform is hollowed out of its original dynamism and appeal, and those left wanting as a result of the impoverishment of the platform and community are left to contemplate an exit strategy with few, if any, redeeming options. 'Enshittification', Doctorow concludes, 'is truly how platforms die'. Doctorow's assessment of modern-day internet culture in Western, Eurocentric, capitalist, and neo-liberal enclaves is useful because it captures the essential hollowness of so much of what passes as internet use, participation, and consumption. Because media platforms have been overridden and subsumed by the neo-liberal logics of platform capitalism (Srnicek 2017), now is as good a time as any to abandon the internet imaginaries of a former era in search of (a) decolonial media option(s). Only by acknowledging the enshittification of digital media and internet platforms can we begin to embark on the formulation, conceptualization, and circulation of new and alternative desire lines.

The internet, decolonized

In 'The internet will be decolonized', Kavita Philip (2021) offers a useful point of departure for exploring the component parts that could lay the foundation for decolonial media imaginaries to emerge. As Philip suggests, the internet can and will be decolonized, and in order for this vision to come to fruition, three overlapping projects must take wing: (1) the democratization of production, dissemination, and ownership of knowledge; (2) the democratization of access to, and governance of, materiality and infrastructure; and (3) the diversification of representation and narrative (2021: 111). Philip argues that the internet is at once structured and shaped by 'historical legacies of colonial ways of knowing, and representing, the world' – to such an extent that 'colonialism and imperialism are now seen as structuring the ways in which internet-based technologies are built, maintained, and used' (2021: 91–92). One of Philip's core concerns is to acknowledge that the political and the digital, as well as the material and ethereal, are inseparable, and as a result, the decolonial project associated with democratizing the ownership, production, and dissemination of knowledge must be connected to larger struggles over the material infrastructures and architectures of the internet. To put things even more concretely, Philip poses the following question regarding internet materiality: 'who labored on these connections, who owns them, who represents them, who benefits from them?' (2021: 112). Thus, questions of labour, matter, environment, education, geopolitics, and representation all serve a crucial role in any future decolonial transformations to come.

The concentration of media ownership is well documented the world over (Noam 2016; Winseck 2022), and critical political economy of the media scholars have shown that 'data, knowledge, expertise, and high-performance infrastructures are kept and mined by an increasingly smaller number of transnational corporations' (Bon et al. 2022: 63). Under this model, we are galaxies away from creating digital infrastructure as a universal service (Thorat 2019: 253). In a representative example of what they refer to as technological coloniality, Bon et al. (2022) describe the expression of power among dominant transnational tech firms as the process of colonizing roles and functions from the state (e.g. education) through a top-down *gifting* of digital services to higher education as a portal to targeting young people and shoring up tax reductions, market penetration, and policy-making influence. To return to Philip's (2021) core questions surrounding who owns and benefits from these infrastructures, it is largely the transnational corporate technology firms that have come to dominate and control on their own terms. One of the most devastating aspects tied to the expansion of technical systems and infrastructures of, for example, the internet, is that these investments 'often create decades or even centuries of path dependencies – meaning that, once built, they continue to shape how we organize society' (Schmelzer et al. 2022: 149). As Dhanashree Thorat (2019: 263–64) has shown, the same inequities exacerbated under the colonial telegraph system of the nineteenth century continue today under the capitalist development of internet infrastructure, with digital infrastructures in India and the Global South developed not for the benefit of (formerly) colonized peoples, but to further the interests of powerful countries in the Global North.

To offer a set of parallel examples, infrastructure such as roads and highways have produced the conditions for cars to dominate cities, superhighways, and suburbs; oil consumption has helped accelerate climate crises making the climate hotter and increasing everyday reliance on oil infrastructures for extraction and consumption to ensure indoor and outdoor spaces remain habitable, let alone comfortable (Schmelzer et al. 2022: 150). Just as the automobile industry and Big Oil have continued to benefit from both the maintenance and expansion of infrastructure and infrastructure-dependent projects, so too have transnational media and technology corporations opted to deepen and intensify their reliance on these systems. And just as automobiles and oil extractivism have been resisted and rejected by various groups and communities across the globe, so too have the latter produced alternative visions and viable alternatives to the hegemonic petrocultures of the present (e.g. pedestrian-only neighbourhoods; bicycle-friendly cities). Similar moves have been made to counter the dominance of the tech and media industries through community-based, grassroots-level infrastructure initiatives. As Ramesh Srinivasan (2019: 239) observes, such community-run projects – such as the creation of mesh networks and Wifi systems – foreground the importance of ownership, design, and maintenance on the part of local communities; within this context, we can situate these initiatives as forays into conceptualizing infrastructure on a human and environmental scale, and as efforts to decentralize technology access and power from the top-down to the bottom-up. Within a decolonial context, interventions would seek to move well beyond resisting the status quo based on everyday enshittification and ever-expansive technological and corporate colonialism in favour of decolonial praxes that reject capitalist regimes of extractivism towards the articulation of a bottom-up rethinking of technology and human collaboration (Causevic et al. 2020: 20). As Marisa Duarte (2017: 129) has shown in her research on digital networks in Indigenous communities, the decolonial involves moving beyond anticolonial critique towards building infrastructures that support Indigenous self-governance and self-determination. The next section of this chapter explores further the decolonial dimensions of this project by shifting obliquely away from digital media infrastructure to consider the potential role solar infrastructural imaginaries could play in supporting Indigenous solidarity, self-governance, and sovereignty.

Indigenous solarities and solar infrastructural imaginaries

> [Solarity] projects are a practice of worldbuilding and futurecasting in resistance to the present energy regime.
>
> (After Oil Collective 2022: 40)

A defining feature of colonial and capitalist exploitation is the colonizer-capitalist framing of nature as less an agent, actor, or organism, and more a 'partner' to be disciplined and controlled under the guise of emancipation. As Mél Hogan writes, the taming of nature 'speaks to long held colonial ideas about controlling nature, managing it as interconnected nodes in a system, and foremost, as requiring human intervention to stay alive for the benefit of humans' (2018: 635). In Canada, a dozen infrastructure projects have participated in the shaping of the national imaginary, among them, the Trans-Canada highway, Canadian Pacific Railroad, electrical, telephone, and postal systems, grain elevators, airways, and airports (Vance cited in Barney 2017: 79). Such projects, Maurice Charland has argued, have contributed to a kind of technological nationalism that works in tandem with an accompanying logic – that 'the popular mind, like the land, must be occupied' (1986: 206). The paradoxical project of so-called nation-building hinges on the politics and ideology that a binding national imaginary can only come into being through massive infrastructure projects driven by capitalist exploitation and private accumulation (Barney 2017: 87).

'We actually need panels not pipelines' – Melina Laboucan-Massimo (Tiny House Warriors 2017)

In terms of upending dominant narratives that centre public infrastructure projects as the sole domain of private interests, the question of solar infrastructure has come to represent a new horizon for reimagining changes to energy infrastructure, human and *extrahuman* relations (see Newell and Pype 2021: 8), and collectivity- and solidarity-oriented practices. The turn towards solar infrastructure among Indigenous communities from different nations has put solidarity, collaboration, and materiality at the forefront of discussions surrounding just energy futures. In a recent work entitled, 'Solar infrastructure as media of resistance, or, Indigenous solarities against settler colonialism', Jordan B. Kinder (2021) explores the generative possibilities at work in two Indigenous-led solar panel community projects – the Piitapan Solar Project and the Tiny House Warriors. Through these examples, Kinder examines the entanglements and affordances that fossil fuel extractivist capitalism have wrought, highlighting the degree to which the settler-colonial state apparatus undermines Indigenous sovereignty, and illustrating how Indigenous communities resist these attempts to further dispossess and undermine Indigenous autonomy. More concretely, both the Piitapan and Tiny House Warriors solar projects can be regarded as efforts to establish 'alternative energetic and infrastructural relations and imaginaries' (2021: 68) in communities deeply impacted by extractivist energy regimes. Completed in 2015, the Piitapan Solar Project consisted of a collaboration between Sacred Earth Solar (SES) and the local Lubicon Cree community, who facilitated the installation of 80 raised solar panels that have served to power the community health centre in Little Buffalo, Alberta (located in the heart of the province's Peace River oil sands). The Tiny House Warriors have also collaborated with SES to build tiny mobile houses equipped with solar infrastructure designed to occupy the paths that dot the massive Trans Mountain Expansion Pipeline Project (TMX). Both respective communities have forged these initiatives as responses to the ecological harm precipitated by catastrophic oil spills (e.g. Little Buffalo in 2011) and as resistance to the ever-encroaching dispossession of Indigenous peoples through extractivist projects like the TMX (2021: 69). Indeed, with every new extractivist project comes the likelihood of real displacement and real environmental destruction.

Kinder's (2021) larger argument is that these solar infrastructural interventions not only produce a critique of, and alternative to, the dominant fossil capital energy regimes of the twentieth and twenty-first centuries, they also create a visible, reproducible, and future-oriented material manifestation of Indigenous resistance through solar infrastructure. 'Indigenous solarities', Kinder suggests, 'are a kind of futurism that fuse solar technologies with Indigenous epistemologies and ways of being to promise a decolonial, just energy future' (2021: 71). As Shannon Speed (2017: 788) has shown, neo-liberal colonialism is marked by its never-ending extractivist projects and defined by its constant enforced subjugation of Indigenous peoples to work on their own expropriated lands for the benefit of capitalist exploitation; such a brutal and dehumanizing project has worked to diminish the sovereignty of Indigenous peoples and to ensure that their dispossession be deemed acceptable. The doublespeak of Canada's Trudeau-led Liberal Government offers a clear example of the state's oppressive presence: in June 2017, Trudeau issued a formal press release on National Aboriginal Day stating that 'no relationship is more important to Canada than the relationship with Indigenous Peoples' – a mere six months after the government approved the TMX pipeline project, a $21.4 billion, 1150 km pipeline projected to carry 300,000 barrels of oil per day from Alberta to the West Coast (Stephenson 2022). In August 2018, a federal court of appeals struck a unanimous decision to halt the TMX due to the government's failure to adequately consult with First Nations communities (Kassam 2018). As Will George, member of the North Vancouver Tsleil-Waututh Nation, has said of Prime Minister Trudeau, 'Climate leaders don't build pipelines' ('Climate leaders'). Offering an important counterpoint to these oppressive realities, Indigenous community-led reorientations towards solar infrastructure have drawn sharp distinctions between infrastructures of foreclosure and possibility, and between regimes of dispossession and sovereign communities. Most importantly, collaborations initiated by Indigenous-led organizations such as Sacred Earth Solar have sparked new imaginaries-work that is giving rise to greater and greater expressions of Indigenous self-determination, and solidifying new pathways to achieving sustainable energy futures.

To date, SES has facilitated three additional solar projects that have served to support art, knowledge, and language revitalization (Nimkii Aazhibikong), as well as housing at Gidimt'en Checkpoint (Wet'suwet'en Territory), and solar panelling at Ada'itsx/Fair Creek to protect Indigenous land defenders and youth (Sacred Earth Solar: n.pag.). These projects have helped sustain Indigenous communities as they care for, protect, and defend their lands and territories against the tremendous pressure and violence inflicted by the settler nation state and the energy industries. Each of the above-mentioned solar projects speak to the modest interventions needed to produce alternative energy imaginaries and to give rise to different kinds of relations between various peoples and the environment, and between communities and energy consumption. Elsewhere in what might be called the rest of Canada, experiments are well underway in attempting to bring about more decentralized, democratically controlled, and sustainably just energy infrastructures through cooperative and community-led groups who hope to contribute, however modestly, to positive social change (After Oil Collective 2022: 57). For Indigenous communities in Canada, however, the stakes for solar infrastructure are much higher, in that the latter represents one of many promising paths towards the realization of Indigenous sovereignty and self-determination. As the After Oil Collective remind us, Indigenous voices must be centred in the elaboration of all projects involving the futures of territories, as well as the futures surrounding land and water use for energy production (2022: 35). Energy infrastructure can and should be reconfigured as a collective and publicly shared good that increases our capacity to live together in community via the sharing of food, shelter, labour, natural resources, and life itself (Wilson 2018: 393). The fact that economic elites and the most powerful institutions of our time continue to argue that they alone possess the knowledge, wherewithal, and means to extract natural resources for the benefit of humanity (Taffel 2023) – without any reference to the unrivalled economic inequality and ecological harm they produce – has meant that the imaginaries-work tied to infrastructural development has been one of myopic foreclosure. What the Indigenous solar imaginaries of the future portend is that visionary infrastructures (Brennan 2017) may soon replace destructive ones in search of better and more just worlds. Having gestured towards the promise and possibilities at work in the solar imaginaries of Indigenous communities and organizations on Turtle Island, I now turn to another form of imaginaries-work that offers a bridge between Indigenous and non-Indigenous community members in Mi'kma'ki (Atlantic Canada).

The running of the salmon as imaginaries-work

In terms of presenting a companion form of imaginaries-work that channels a decolonial ethos, Sylvia Moore's (2017b) work in *Trickster Chases the Tale of Education* represents a vital point of departure for advancing the decolonial through the interrelated lenses of land, education, community, and relations. Sylvia Moore is an educational researcher living and working in Mi'kma'ki, in what represents the northeastern region of Turtle Island. For settlers in the region, this part of the world is most commonly referred to as Atlantic Canada. Moore's richly woven story chronicles a collaboration between the Indigenous community of Wildcat First Nation and the primary-secondary rural school of North Queens, an initiative that spawned (quite literally) a salmon project in the community, as well as the implementation of a Native studies course in the school. The story begins in 2007 when Moore acquired salmon eggs from a local fish hatchery with the view that the salmon would be raised in the school, thereby enabling the students to witness and learn from the hatching process (Moore 2017a). During this time, Moore was approached by Wildcat First Nation who offered to host the release of the 300 salmon, inviting elementary students and school staff to participate in a ceremony that included smudging, drumming, and prayers (2017b: 10). In the winter of 2008, a second iteration of the salmon project was proposed, only this time it would be situated in Wildcat First Nation. The project was conceived to be centred in the Mi'kmaw community so as to foreground Mi'kmaw understandings of the world and to legitimate Mi'kmaw knowledge, with an eye towards moving 'an Aboriginal education agenda forward' (2017b: 10). Shifting the project's location from the school to the Mi'kmaw community signalled a deeper issue to be addressed during the project – the 'tear in the fabric of relations among people' – namely, between members of the Indigenous and non-Indigenous community. To be sure, one of the chief concerns expressed prior to the beginning of the 2008 project was the perceived rift between Indigenous and non-Indigenous community members. For example, it was not recommended that the project take place in the school because Indigenous parents were not comfortable entering schools (see TRC's expansive reports on Canada's Residential Schools); yet another expression of the rift was the perception among settlers (or non-Indigenous people) that they were not welcome on the Mi'kmaw reservations.

Thus, to situate the project within the Mi'kmaw community represented an opportunity to bring the school into the community, and to extend an even broader invitation to non-community members in the interests of repairing injury and restoring relations. Moore's doctoral research was carried out in collaboration with the Mi'kmaw community and a dedicated group of co-researchers, Elders, and Traditional Knowledge Keepers, in a process that is perhaps best encapsulated here: 'Together we had learned about the salmon, told stories, listened to one another, shared food, learned, and released the salmon. To simply be together and share in the salmon project was a sign of improved relationships among people' (2017b: 51). The community participated in weekly learning circles designed to facilitate the sharing of stories and a deeper understanding of the salmon. Through these weekly 'experiences of living, learning, and relationship' (2017b: 19), the broader community was afforded the opportunity to gather around the tank, smudge, tell stories, share food, sing, drum, and observe the salmon. For Moore, the salmon project is as much about reclaiming Indigenous identity, tradition, and education, as it is about enhancing relations, rejuvenating, and replenishing the people and the salmon (2017b: 41).

Trickster Chases the Tale of Education participates in meaningful decolonial imaginaries-work through three interconnected strands: ecological/environmental, relational, and experiential/ontological (see Figure 3.1). One of the most pressing concerns articulated in the book surrounds the disappearance of the salmon in the region. The question of why the salmon left looms large from the outset. Did they leave due to the river dams, polluted waters, or overfishing? In a telling dream sequence, a silvery black salmon explains to Moore (2017b: 33) that although the project involving humans talking about the salmon is important and reparative, the reality remains that humans lack care and reciprocity towards the fish and the rivers. Indeed, the lack of care and reciprocity towards the salmon is enacted through the building of dams, the polluting of waters, and the practices of overfishing and overconsumption. Related to the ecological and environmental concerns expressed above is the notion that members of the broader community have failed to live up to their responsibilities to other creatures and species. Building on theologian George Tinker's work, Moore affirms that merely stating

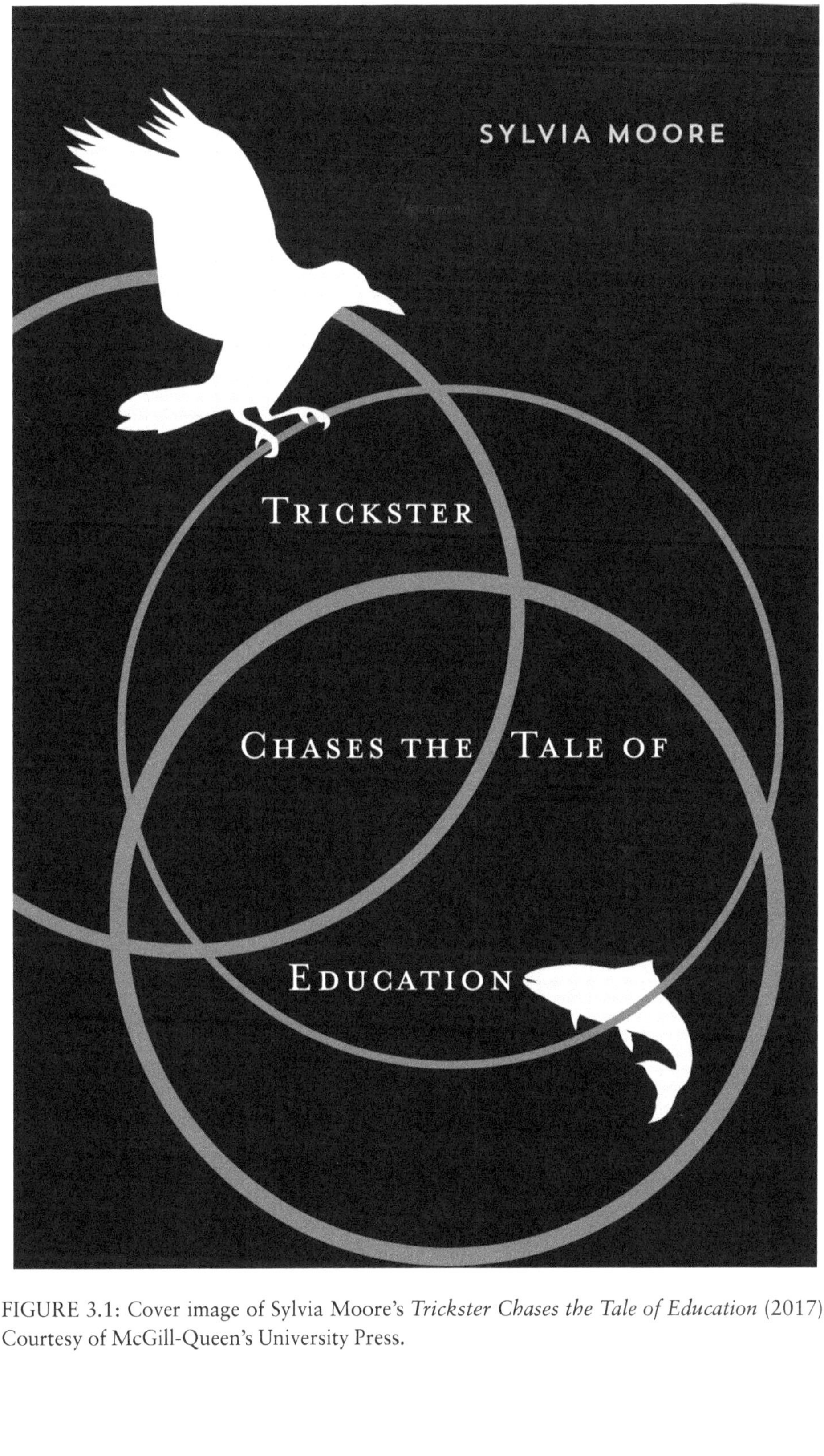

FIGURE 3.1: Cover image of Sylvia Moore's *Trickster Chases the Tale of Education* (2017). Courtesy of McGill-Queen's University Press.

'we are all related' does not go far enough to ensure mutual flourishing and interconnectivity within the Web of Life. Rather, Moore asks her readers to consider the environmental impacts associated with everyday practices such as lighting a room or heating the water – electricity produced by the damming of a river renders it impossible for salmon to travel certain rivers, thereby impeding opportunities to spawn. Importantly, the salmon project produces even deeper ecological resonances with the release of salmon, a process culminating with the return of 300 salmon to their natal river. This rejuvenation of the salmon population serves as a corrective to previous historical lapses in responsibility and care. The tension between human arrogance and non-human marginalization takes pride of place in Moore's problematization of existing relations, and although these tensions never fully dissolve, the salmon project is successful in reducing human irresponsibility and improving visibility for the more-than-human.

The salmon project is a veritable instance of a community confronting the absence of care and responsibility towards the environment, at the same time that it is an invitation to re-centre relations and to nurture relationships anew. The undertaking evolved into a collaboratively constructed story fostered through respect and reciprocity and fashioned in the interests of restoring human and more-than-human relationships (Moore 2017b: 120). On a basic level, the talking circles were crucial to developing a shared acknowledgement of the salmon's important role in sustaining families and community. Sharing stories about the salmon became a prominent feature of the talking circles – talk of the size and quantity of the salmon during one's childhood, memories of catching and eating salmon in cherished locations, oral stories, and traditions connecting salmon with the people and the land. The invitation to have Indigenous and non-Indigenous community members (comprised of students, school staff, Wildcat First Nation members, and settlers) participate in the salmon project added depth and significance to a project that might have otherwise been restricted to a much smaller group of collaborators. The project could have been limited to any of the following groups and locations: the research team led by Moore; the Wildcat First Nation community store, the North Queens School. The decision to include as many of these actors and groups as possible demonstrates not only a concerted commitment to and cultivation of relations, but it also affirms that these methods can have a galvanizing impact on disparate communities that may not always have the space, room, time, energy, resources, or wherewithal to come together. As Moore (2017a) recounts, talking circle participants may have loosely recognized one another initially, but they did not know each other; that said, these weekly gatherings afforded group members the opportunity to come to know one another through listening, relating to, and being in relationship together. For a time, the salmon project would propel community members into collective relationships based on reciprocity through a process that would serve to 'spin the web of connections even larger' (2017b: 76); put another way, this undertaking constitutes 'relationship work' that privileges 'nurturing and restoring good and right relations' (2017b: 121). Importantly, these imaginaries cannot be adequately understood solely via visual representations associated with, for example, Sacred Earth Solar's YouTube presence, or, the DVD videos created by North Queens students, but rather through a confluence of competing accounts concerning the vibrant future paths needed to ensure collective flourishing.

The salmon project also holds enormous potential for thinking about decolonial imaginaries for its capacity to incite and instil various kinds of refusal and resistance. At the heart of this project is the desire, however gently articulated, to overturn colonial and capitalist forms of hegemony that have created environmental and community-based harm. Moore's motivations as educator and researcher are clearly defined: to push an Indigenous education agenda forward and to decentre Eurocentric knowledge as the basis upon which all education is based or conceived. Importantly, *Trickster* advances this project not by merely championing Indigenous worldviews at the expense of Western epistemologies; rather, the book centres Indigenous perspectives and ways of knowing at the same time that it grapples with the legacies of colonialism within and beyond the education system. One helpful mode of intervention introduced by Moore is Albert Marshall's concept of Two-Eyed Seeing, in what can be characterized as a yoking together of Indigenous and Eurocentric knowledge systems or worldviews. According to Marshall, a vital component of this confluence between Eurocentric and Indigenous worldviews is to 'respect the differences between the two perspectives and to focus on, and work from, a position of shared strengths' (Marshall cited in Moore 2017b: 114). Moore's work in the school – especially in her incorporation of a Native studies course – constitutes her stated investment in the dismantling of colonialism via education, in what she otherwise refers to as the 'decolonizing work in education' (2017b: 10). Connected to this larger project of decolonization is the desire to resist the 'default thinking patterns' (2017b: 100–01) that are the hallmark of colonial education models. Moore herself addresses the challenges of being locked into her own default thought patterns in her research and in everyday life. Through her communion with nature, family, and community, she is able to negotiate these barriers in her thinking, the fruits of which are expressed through her dynamic writing: the book channels Indigenous methodologies, Mi'kmaw storytelling, decolonial pedagogy, Indigenous knowledge, trickster dialogues, and dream sequences. As far as experiential and ontological changes can be perceived, Moore's desired transformations within the education system and the community 'will grow in its own time' (2017b: 125). Change on this level can be seen in the short term via other means: once the Wildcat First Nation project came to fruition, Indigenous band councillors expressed interest in taking on their own salmon projects, and more teachers and community members agreed to organize an annual salmon project as part of advancing Indigenous education forward. Investments and commitments of this kind emphasize the slow but concerted nature of integrating new and/or traditional ways of living and being into the fold of a community, all the while recognizing that change of this kind evolves slowly.

In drawing this chapter to a useful conclusion, I want to pose the following question: what can infrastructural solarities projects and the running of the salmon project do to expand our understanding of media and the decolonial? In juxtaposing the latter two examples with the materialist, political-economic, extractivist, and neocolonial imperatives at work in the fullest expression of corporate-capitalist media interests, I have attempted to highlight how the imaginaries-work of these groups matters in both the short- and long-term visions to be articulated for the future. In the case of dominant media interests, the realization of their imaginaries will always serve to proliferate and reproduce visions of progress that simultaneously uphold an elite-friendly status quo and deepen the already overflowing coffers of the world's wealthiest few. In the case of Indigenous interests, imaginaries-work represents a vital facet of the wilful fulfilment of future-oriented projects that centre community, collectivity, and reciprocity. The work of sustainable energy generation and decolonial-oriented community relations and education proposes a different kind of imaginaries-work capable of advancing the possibility of good and right relations, just futures, and community sovereignty. The next chapter addresses the role a specific set of actors, decolonial scholars, play in the articulation of decolonial futures.

4

Decolonial Scholars, Decolonial Futures

In the preceding chapter, I explored the possibility of advancing good and right relations, just futures, and community sovereignty by way of imaginaries-work both within and beyond Indigenous community frameworks. The discussion surrounding infrastructural solarities and running of the salmon projects as community-centred initiatives developed by Indigenous communities was presented as a form of imaginaries-creation capable of redirecting collective energies away from colonial and capitalist ways of perceiving and inhabiting the world, and towards regenerative and reparative worldbuilding activities in the pockets and places in which we dwell most. In this chapter, I shift the discussion from infrastructural horizons to institutional potentialities through the exploration of a different site of contestation over the creation and proliferation of imaginaries-work – the neo-liberal university. Motivated by my positionality and subjectivity as a university worker and settler academic, I now turn to the university as an important site for thinking about not only the work of decolonial politics, but also for exploring the labour of university workers as a more elaborate case study for reflecting on the cultivation and implementation of new desire lines and/or lines of flight for challenging, subverting, or steering institutions towards decolonization efforts. University workers – students, staff, and faculty – are not, by default, predisposed to engaging in the elaboration of institutional critique or reform, but there is nonetheless a rich history of critique and reform from within and beyond the university that may serve as a compass or reorientation device for decolonial change and transformation.

I begin with la paperson's (2017) call for university workers to participate in the elaboration of a *third university* as a point of departure for reflecting on the decolonial politics needed to bring about decolonial futures. In *A Third University Is Possible*, paperson argues that the modern-day university is charged with bringing about the rematriation of land, and with furthering the project of anticolonialism, in what would constitute a seismic reversal of 'the colonizing machine's [the university's] desires to settle, to self-sustain, to seduce, and to school' (2017: xxii). For these futures to materialize, a profound reckoning must occur across and beyond the institution. US and Canadian land-grant universities of the nineteenth century were most adept in accumulating land, converting Indigenous lands into capital, converting capital into institutions, and converting land into agriculture and agribusiness (paperson 2017: 28; Kauffman 2023: 181). The university systems of the present exist as emblematic expressions of settler-colonialism: they have and continue to participate in the dispossession of peoples, the expropriation of lands, and the expansion of settler rights and protections, in what amounts to a troubling legacy that has produced unspeakable forms of alienation between Black and Indigenous peoples, between humans and more-than-humans, between land and life (paperson 2017: 4). It is crucial to note that the third university paperson proposes is more invested in operating as a decolonizing university and less interested in merely decolonizing the university (2017: 53). As paperson sees it, the figure of the *scyborg* (his neologism) – a central actor already embedded in the university system – occupies a privileged position to assemble decolonizing machines for the purposes of plugging the university into decolonizing assemblages (see 'You, a scyborg' chapter). If the neo-liberal university of the current moment is plugged into military-industrial and corporate-capitalist assemblages (to name but two), the work required to redirect these assemblages towards decolonizing ends is as broad as it is expansive.

In what follows, I highlight specific forms of institutional critique and reform within and beyond the university as potential sites for decolonial change and transformation. This chapter thus situates the work of Indigenous, postcolonial, feminist, and critical media studies thinkers to put forward a more coherent picture of the contradictions, counter-forces, and solidarities that underpin the struggle for decolonial futures. To guide the discussion, I engage the following two questions: (1) What elements are needed to bring decolonial imaginaries into being? (2) What are some of the possible moves to be made on the part of decolonial scholars in the shift towards decolonial futures? In exploring these questions directly, I look to engage Denise da Silva's affirmation that 'we cannot stay in the work of critique, but we must go *through* critique to get to the work' (cited in paperson 2017: 43, original emphasis); I also seek to channel Sabelo J. Ndlovu-Gatsheni's provocation that reworlding projects may only ever advance through 'a double move of critique and reconstitution' (2023: 2259). In exploring these lines of inquiry, I hope to identify useful through lines and points of connection for university workers getting to the work of decolonial politics.

Elements

The running of the salmon and infrastructural solarities projects of the previous chapter invite the formation of new sensibilities in the elaboration of decolonial imaginaries-work. Having already described some of the attendant features and dynamics embedded within these two very different decolonial projects, I now turn to a much broader discussion of the elements needed to bring about decolonial imaginaries. One vital element associated with this project has to do with the language used to describe the world we currently inhabit. For Natalie Loveless, *end-of-the-world* language has been mobilized of late to describe not an apocalyptic endpoint for people or the planet per se, but rather as the end of *a* world 'under petrocultural colonial capitalism and anthropocentric humanism' (2019: 99). If we accept that the current petrocultural, colonial, capitalist, and anthropocentric order of things continues to punish and disenfranchise a vast swath of the world's human and more-than-human population, then the call to bring about transformation is as urgent as it is welcome. As Donna Haraway eloquently puts it, what is needed are 'on the ground collectives capable of new practices of imagination, resistance, revolt, repair, and mourning and living and dying well' (2016: 51). As Haraway sees it, social transformation must be won, bit by bit, against the grain of dominant capitalist cultures to make room for new possibilities of living and dying well.

Visions for how to bring these new worlds into being differ. As Candace Fujikane (2021: 11) has shown, a fundamental facet of this project lies in dislodging the roots of occupation and in dismantling settler colonial logics and capitalist economies of scarcity. The Indigenous communities of Hawai'i (Kanaka Maoli) that Fujikane chronicles have long resisted 'the occupying state and developers['s efforts to] represent wondrous lands as wastelands' (2021: 63) for the sole purposes of extraction and development. Instead, Kanaka Maoli have cultivated relations premised on interconnectedness that place land and water protection at the forefront of community activist movements. In so doing, they have sought to map the abundance people create in conjunction with the land through, for example, the renewal of ancestral fishponds, the restoration of seaweed, and the revitalization and repair of waterways. Fujikane's work offers a powerful set of examples that simultaneously illustrate the rejection of dominant forms of capitalist enclosure as well as the championing of Indigenous practices of attunement towards ecological and environmental forms of abundance. Companion restoration and conservation projects abound at the current moment, many of which hold space to foreground the immediacy of our dystopian present, all the while introducing Indigenous practices, stories, relations, and knowledges in such a way as to bring into being new sustainable futures. On the one hand, Kyle Whyte (2017) situates the dystopia experienced by Indigenous communities over hundreds of years as a by-product of ongoing colonial oppression; on the other hand, he counterbalances these histories with regenerative conservation projects geared towards the restabilization of Nmé (fish), manoomin (wild rice) and nibi (water). As Whyte explains, projects of this nature lay bare 'how industrial settler campaigns erase the particular systems of interdependent relationships of humans, nonhumans, and ecosystems that matter to many indigenous peoples' (2017: 213), just as much as they remind us that Indigenous communities respond to dystopian contexts by applying knowledge as a means to survive and flourish. For both Fujikane and Whyte, Indigenous communities are propelled to navigate harmful colonial and capitalist contexts in order to map better, more abundant, and regenerative futures. Perhaps the greatest anomaly to emerge from the centuries-long destructive cycles spurred along by colonial and capitalist conquest is that 'those peoples thought to be "under-developed" may hold the keys to future survival' (Fenelon and Alford 2020: 389).

In similar fashion, Leanne Betasamosake Simpson's work as a Nishnaabeg artist, writer, and scholar emphasizes the notion that decolonial transformation requires the abolition of capitalism and heteropatriarchy, as well as a reckoning with and remaking of every aspect of life among a diversity of living beings; in her view, this would entail acting according to a Nishnaabeg imperative and way of life, one that privileges reciprocal practices of taking only what one needs, making use of everything one takes, sharing everything one has, and promoting the flourishing of life (Maynard and Simpson 2022: 180–81). Simpson argues that intellectual knowledge is not enough of its own accord in the face of centuries of settler occupation and gendered violence – rather, embodiment and lived experience, consensual relations, and attunement to the land as pedagogy, all have a part to play in decolonial moves towards Nishnaabeg resurgence (Simpson 2014: 16). Intrinsic to the flourishing described by Simpson is the collectivity of both human and more-than-human species. By way of offering a grounding example, Robin Wall Kimmerer (2013) refers to the power of unity and collectivity expressed by trees: the latter participate in both a weave and a chain of reciprocity with the soil, fungus, squirrels, and human beings, among countless other species. Through their reciprocal acts of collectivity, Kimmerer (2013: 21) conveys the powerful idea that 'all flourishing is mutual', reminding us that fostering multispecies care and interdependence constitutes a vital element in bringing about decolonial ways of being. Both Simpson and Kimmerer's concerns resonate clearly in the work of Anna Tsing, who, in *The Mushroom at the End of the World*, contends with the dire reality that 'we are stuck with the problem of living despite economic and ecological ruination. Neither tales of progress nor of ruin tell us how to think about collaborative survival' (2015: 19). Tsing is not only interested in exploring worldmaking projects arising out of ruination and expressed through human and more-than-human assemblages (e.g. foragers-mushrooms-soil-trees), she is also interested in complicating how notions of human progress have obscured ties across multispecies environments. As Tsing asserts, we may very well have reached 'the end of expectations of progress aimed toward collective advancement' (2015: 110), but imagination and collaboration may hold the key to future mutual flourishing and survival.

To say goodbye to unjust worlds in preparation for new liveable ones is to conceive of life as lived according to a different set of relations. A lingering obstacle to the advancement of futures beyond the sunset of capitalism and heteropatriarchy is the failure to collectively imagine the world otherwise. Contemporary crises spurred on by economic inequality, climate injustice, and political uncertainty create more than enough friction and chaos to cloud over and enclose the collective imagination, a phenomenon that has created a veritable lag in the conjuring of new worlds and relations. Social movement scholars Max Haiven and Alex Khasnabish (2014) explore this phenomenon at length in *The Radical Imagination*, in which they contextualize and make sense of the pressures and forces that limit activists, communities, and social movements from furthering collective goals for radical social change and towards better futures. Haiven and Khasnabish (2014: 61) invoke the term the 'radical imagination' to represent 'the ability to envision and work towards better futures based on an analysis of the root causes of social problems' – and it is precisely this ability to imagine the world otherwise that is atrophying more generally under the weight of the deepening crises exacerbated both prior to and post-COVID-19 pandemic. It is important to note that Haiven and Khasnabish have made concerted efforts to study the bleak moments and historic low points activist communities have faced – what they refer to as 'dwelling in the hiatus' – as examples of how groups and communities can 'dwell between not-success and not-failure' as a strategy for sustaining solidarity and persistence (2014: 488).

Whatever the highs, mids, or lows experienced by various communities, the question of how to live, survive, and flourish in the midst of sustained precarity the world over is only partially attended to through efforts to nourish the collective imagination. In *Light in the Dark*, Gloria Anzaldúa confronts the crushing reality that human beings have become all too familiar and comfortable with 'colonialism's wounds' (2015: 44). According to Anzaldúa, part of the healing process involves prolonged efforts to dismantle one's grounded identity and subjectivity – 'You'll have to leave parts of yourself behind' (2015: 137) – combined with sustained endeavours to 'be in conocimiento' with others (sharing knowledge, pooling resources, confronting institutional power, processing, and healing wounds) (2015: 91). As Avtar Brah has suggested, the cultivation of a 'cosmopolitan imagination helps illuminate local and global connections and a cosmopolitan sensibility enhances the capacity for care and obligation to others' (2022: 211). In her view, imagination and care must be coupled and combined to enhance relations and to nurture the political possibilities at the heart of alliance- and coalition-building (2022: 201). In orienting ourselves more to the cultivation of relations grounded in care and obligation, we deepen the possibilities of 'living with', that is, of initiating a shift from matters of concern to matters of care (Puig de la Bellacasa 2017). Kristina Lindström and Åsa Ståhl (2020: 137, 146) have suggested that 'living with' represents an invitation to relate – practically, affectively, and ethically – to matter, objects, and others in such a way as to sensitize us to new entanglements and interdependencies. Care may be necessary, but it is certainly not a given; add to this the sobering reality that care work is defined by the asymmetries of reciprocity that punctuate the majority of caring relations (Puig de la Bellacasa 2017: 121). Despite these asymmetries, both care and care work constitute 'an ethical social relationship based on both feelings of affection and a sense of service' (Dowling 2021: 64), as well as a set of priorities and commitments that together serve as a foundational element associated with flourishing and living well. For Carol A. Taylor (2020: 260), care creates the conditions that 'render the other more capable', thereby unlocking the relational capacities between people and among groups. It may be the case that rather than merely 'living with' as a decolonial orientation, we may need to usher in new arrangements that see living on, after, and with – not to mention living in solidarity and affinity with – as the most viable ways forward (Cooppan 2019: 413).

Moves

In the previous section, I have attempted to conjure an assemblage of elements that may be generative in bringing decolonial imaginaries closer into being. Foundational to this work is the notion of invoking *end-of-the-world* imaginaries in ways that acknowledge capitalism and heteropatriarchy are reaching an inevitable end, and that new imaginaries must inform the basis of our imaginings for better future worlds. The *elements* to be imbricated in this broader set of decolonial assemblages are vital to this project of reworlding and otherworlding, but some discussion of the moves (and movements) to be made on this front are also essential to setting decolonial futures in motion.

I begin the discussion surrounding the possible moves to be made on this front through two related instances of explicit decolonial institutional critique – the first of which took root in Cape Town, South Africa; the second in Oxford, England. In March 2015, Chumani Maxwele, a Black student at the University of Cape Town (UCT), publicly defiled a bronze statue of white British imperialist Cecil John Rhodes located in the centre of the university campus. Maxwele's call for the removal of white supremacist iconography from campus was made palpable through emptying a bucket of human faeces over the statue (Hall 2015).

As A. Kayum Ahmed has remarked, Maxwele and other UCT students would soon after ignite the #RhodesMustFall (#RMF) movement, 'a radical student movement centred on decolonizing UCT by confronting questions of institutional racism, increasing access to education, and reforming the Eurocentric university curriculum' (2020: 282). Whereas members of the UCT student collective called for (and a month later were granted) the removal of the statue (see Figure 4.1), the most important dimensions of their work materialized as part of their explicit demands to decolonize the institution through policy and curriculum change. The #RMF campaign would go on to inspire solidarity actions in both the United States and the United Kingdom, most notably at Oxford University. Although both respective student campaigns can be seen to have been engaging in acts of 'epistemic disobedience' (Mignolo 2009) and in calls to decolonize the university, marked differences emerged in the articulation of each group's critiques of the institution. As Ahmed (2020: 285, 296) illustrates, there are degrees of epistemic disobedience, a point neatly distilled through the Oxford and Cape Town case studies: Oxford student activists were invested in achieving three core goals – to remove colonial iconography, replace Eurocentric curriculum, and dismantle racial inequalities; whereas the Oxford student movement sought to integrate marginal ideas into the

FIGURE 4.1: The removal of the Cecil John Rhodes statue on the University of Cape Town campus on 9 April 2015. Photo by Michael Hammond/University of Cape Town.

existing curriculum, the UCT student movement was far more radical in demanding marginalized epistemologies be centred in the Eurocentric curriculum. The UCT and Oxford campaigns reflect emergent desires on the part of students to engage in radical decolonial politics at universities in the Global South and the Global North, for which the goals, playbooks, and necessities appear to be simultaneously aligned and disjointed. Indeed, the exigencies and urgencies of Cape Town students are not the same as those of Oxford students, nor are their theoretical frames and lived experiences. One valuable insight to be gleaned from both #RhodesMustFall campaigns is that student activist praxis can create avenues for practice to inform and build theory (Ahmed 2020). As Ndlovu-Gatsheni (2018: 8) remarks, #RMF is emblematic of ongoing protests against 'coloniality-at-large' – a state of affairs that has prompted UCT activists to reaffirm their calls to decolonize the university: 'What the students are demanding is the decolonization of the very idea of the university, its institutional culture, management style and epistemological foundations so as to attain cognitive justice' (Ndlovu-Gatsheni 2018: 238). Hence, the actions initiated by UCT and Oxford students offer a useful entry point for exploring the decolonial moves and pathways proposed by actors seeking to contribute to the university's transformation.

Much has already been written on the urgent need to resist the capitalist colonization of academia and to subvert university capitalism (Santos 2018: 356), as it is currently expressed through neo-liberal agendas across the higher education spectrum. Calls to decolonize the mind, knowledge, curricula, academia, and the university are longstanding (Fuchs and Fuchs 2022: 63), as evidenced historically by the wide variety of initiatives dedicated to this project. Yet another key facet to this work is generating 'a material infrastructure of research and higher education' (Fuchs and Fuchs 2022: 73) that supports the work of decolonization. Because this book is less about the decolonization of dominant institutions such as the university and more about the processes and practices of decolonial politics within these dominant institutions, I will pivot towards the latter over the former. Whereas reaching a decisive end point to decolonization ultimately 'requires the repatriation of Indigenous land and life' (Tuck and Yang 2012: 21), it remains to be seen what kinds of decolonial moves may contribute to the fulfilment of this work.

Sara Ahmed's recent work in *What's the Use?* (2019) and *Complaint!* (2021) describes the university (and institutional life, more generally) as akin to the experience of confronting a series of blockages in perpetuity via brick walls and closing doors. In both texts, Ahmed (2021: 154) painstakingly attends to the gaps between how the university appears (a positive environment) and how it is experienced (a hostile environment). As Ahmed shows, universities are prone to valuing institutional order and hierarchy, devaluing the work of those seeking to transform the institution for the better, and coopting the efforts of diversity workers to present claims that they are engaging in diversity work. Among the many insights Ahmed offers, she underlines two aspects that are tied to the trappings of decolonizing the university: reproducing the system and coopting the work/er/s. According to Ahmed, the engines of institutional and social reproduction have much to teach us about the maintenance and perpetuation of undesirable status quos: on the one hand, '[a] system is reproduced by rewarding those who are willing to reproduce the system' (2021: 100), while on the other hand, '[t]rying to address an institutional problem often means inhabiting the institution *all the more*' (2021: 275–76, original emphasis). Issuing a press release that states that the university is engaging in Equity, Diversity, Inclusion, and Accessibility (EDIA) work and/or the work of decolonization (via curriculum, for example) is often justification enough for the university to say that it is engaging in EDIA and decolonization efforts. Silvia Rivera Cusicanqui refers to *gatopardismo* as a useful term of illumination on this front – a concept used to describe 'the policy of changing everything so that everything remains the same' (2020: 57). To participate in the creation of decolonial cracks and fissures (Walsh 2023) requires some acknowledgement that the colonial, capitalist, and neo-liberal system of higher education we have inherited has and will continue to reward those who are willing to reproduce the system, and that those trying to address this (and other) institutional problem(s) will be exposed to the banality, violence, and hostility that are provoked when attempts to make decolonial change materialize.

At their worst, universities participate in the widespread appropriation of Indigenous and other forms of marginalized knowledge through the prism of Western epistemological systems to advance settler colonial priorities (Simpson 2014: 22). Ongoing efforts of this kind have been instrumentalized in such a way as to establish the 'positional superiority of Western knowledge', to colonize the disciplines, and to discipline the colonized (Smith 2021). Universities of the Global North poach knowledge freely from the Global South, with little (if any) acknowledgement of where ideas, methods, approaches, or resources may have originated. Rivera Cusicanqui refers to the North's brazen activities as impoverished forms of mimesis and cooptation that nourish fashionable and depoliticized knowledges:

> Ideas run, like rivers, from the south to the north and are transformed into tributaries in major waves of thought. But just as in the global market for material goods, ideas leave the country converted into raw material, which become regurgitated and jumbled in the final product.
>
> (2020: 63)

These larger forces have been successful in maintaining the hegemony of Eurocentric knowledge within the university system, establishing a political economy of knowledge (Rivera Cusicanqui 2020: 60) or geopolitics of knowledge (Mignolo 2002) that devalues and invisibilizes knowledge from the Global South and champions Western epistemologies. As recently as a decade ago, Mark Graham's work on the geographies of information and knowledge through academic publishing revealed 'some very uneven patterns' (2014: 101) between North America/Western Europe and the African continent; Switzerland, for example, had three times as many journals published than all of Africa. Graham sums up the stakes of these huge epistemological inequalities in these terms: 'with the Global North producing, consuming, and controlling much of the world's codified knowledge, [the] Global South [is] largely left out of these processes' (2014: 103). What's more, universities of the north are more than adept at attracting researchers from the south, only to participate in the eventual cooptation and incorporation of 'new entrants' looking to engage in decolonial work (Keet 2019: 206; Moyo 2020: 173–85). It is perhaps unsurprising that an 'entire "decolonial industry" is now operating to generate social and cultural capital that circles back to cultural institutions to maintain and amplify their hegemonic status' (yamomo and Beyer 2024: 196). Paraphrasing Max Liboiron (2021: 136), the question thus becomes, how do we do our research in the spaces between/among Indigenous knowledge creation pursuits, Euro-Western epistemological paradigms, and neocolonial structures?

One of the most contested areas of discussion in higher education has to do with the reimagining of new university paradigms. Stopping short of calling for the abolition of the university and a full-scale exodus from the job and experience of university life and work (Moten and Harney 2020), many have called for a reconceptualization of the university and its constitution. For some, a good start would be to radically democratize the processes of learning, teaching, research, and scholarship, and to wrest the latter from the corporate university model into something more akin to the spirit of de- and un-schooling initiatives (Haiven and Khasnabish 2014: 252). Arguments for advancing knowledge from the Global South continue with greater and greater frequency (Comaroff and Comaroff 2012; Mignolo 2021a; Moyo 2020; Moyo 2024; Ndlovu-Gatsheni 2018) precisely because a recalibration of epistemological inequalities will help bring forward critical social theory and practice capable of addressing 'the as yet unresolved social challenges of the twenty-first century' (Hayes et al. 2021: 888) – to say nothing of the decolonial politics that stand to emerge from these shifts. Far from merely instrumentalizing students as labourers and knowledge as capital, universities could be reconceived as training grounds for mentoring 'effective healers, imaginers, repairers, transitioners, re/designers, weavers, and caretakers of the mesh of life' (Escobar 2022: 195). In order to accomplish these feats, calls for the university to be decolonized have been made to begin the process of creating 'a less provincial and more open critical cosmopolitan pluriversalism' (Mbembe 2019:

242). The creation of pluriversities (Newell and Pype 2021: 19) and the elaboration of cosmopolitan pluriversalism have gone hand-in-hand with the desire to reconceptualize the university as plastic and elastic. As André Keet (2019: 213) has argued, the university is best conceived of as a plastic (read: malleable) entity innately capable of bringing about its own transformation – a shift towards resolving epistemic injustices, foregrounding undisciplined knowledge, and forging new paths for decolonial politics.

The larger point I wish to make here is that calls to transform the institution are never-ending, and the language used to describe desired transformations is broad and varied. That said, one generative frame for embarking on the work of transforming the institution has to do with the notion of reckoning. Given the enormity and magnitude of attempting to decolonize society, calls for personal and collective reckoning have added much-needed clarity to some of the micro-level work to be done at the decolonial level. Within the realm of higher education, to answer the call for broader reckoning is to deviate from the well-worn paths of institutionally approved status quos. As Ahmed insists, such alternative path-making is fraught and onerous: 'Other paths can be created by being used: use does not make deviation impossible. Deviation is hard. Deviation is made hard' (2019: 42). Members of the university community who refuse to toe the line – who refuse to carry on as though the capitalist, neo-liberal, higher education system is worth preserving – are faced with having to acknowledge that engaging in decolonization efforts is ultimately to recognize one's complicity in 'upholding colonial power structures' (Sundar and Mukherjee 2022: 12). Not only is deviation (made) hard, to reckon with the legacies of settler colonialism is not a superficial, surface-level undertaking, but it is often treated as such. For Tuck and Yang, writing in 2012, the term decolonization had already been in the process of being 'superficially adopted into education and other social sciences' – with its broader adoption and inclusion among many as a manifestation of 'settler moves to innocence', that is, as attempts to 'reconcile settler guilt and complicity and [to] rescue settler futurity' (2012: 2, 3). Even the most well-intentioned, ethical, and conscientious allies risk trivializing, undermining, or sabotaging decolonial efforts by virtue of their close proximity to colonial power structures and reward systems. The work to undo settler guilt and complicity is a complex long-term endeavour bereft of any proven guides, maps, or compasses to lead the way. And yet, complicity can also be viewed not as 'something negative to be resisted and disavowed but [as] something to be affirmed in order to assume responsibility' (Singh 2017: 120). Acknowledging complicity and assuming responsibility represent important moves in reckoning towards decolonial futures in that they can help pave the way for recasting entire worlds.

In *How to Do Nothing*, artist and writer Jenny Odell (2019) offers a promising direction with which to make some headway. She argues that we need to develop a 'vocabulary of refusal' that will incite us to withdraw our attention from dominant imaginaries and reinvest it elsewhere: 'What is needed, then, is not a "once-and-for-all" type of quitting but ongoing training: the ability not just to withdraw attention, but to invest it somewhere else, to enlarge and proliferate it, to improve its acuity' (2019: 68, 93). The long road towards decolonial reckoning involves the transformation of one's relational ties, orientations, commitments, and investments (Singh 2017; Ahmed 2006). More concretely, Sundar and Mukherjee (2022: 5) have suggested that feminist scholars might envisage the decolonial as a form of 'disciplinary reorientation' that could bring about 'greater reflexivity, an accounting of privilege, a defamiliarizing and dismantling of our usual intellectual and disciplinary "habits"'. For scholars, more generally, this can take the form of refusing to uphold mastery as a disciplinary and epistemological ideal, opting instead for a practice of 'vulnerable engagement' that enables them to open themselves up to 'other discourses, peoples, beings, languages (that we know and do not yet know)' (Singh 2017: 90–91). For academics and intellectuals, it can also mean performing epistemic disobedience, delinking from Western epistemology, and unravelling neo-liberal subjectivity (Mignolo and Walsh 2018). For university workers, the privileged figure of the *scyborg* – an already deeply entrenched actor within the institution – is capable of dedicating time, energy, skills, and labour (read: strategies, tools, tactics, and praxis) towards the creation of a third university, giving rise to a redirection of resources and energies towards the soldering of decolonial scraps and assemblages that may help redefine the university as a decolonizing force for the future (paperson 2017).

Suffice it to say that all of the above moves, whatever their power to inspire or instigate, appear more abstract and intangible than they do grounded and workable. Hence, praxis may offer another window into the decolonial politics of the moment, with particular emphasis on the ways in which praxis is being mobilized in higher education. On a fundamental level, this could mean that universities should make possible a more comprehensive integration and inclusion of Indigenous knowledges and perspectives on, for example, land, water, health, rights, and identities (Stoltz et al. 2021: 15). Such a project would not simply equate to surface-level efforts to *indigenize* or *decolonize* existing course, programme, or degree offerings. Such a project would take seriously the work of distinguishing between decolonizing curriculum and merely diversifying it. As Roopika Risam's work attests, the diversification of curriculum can and does serve an important role in 'decentering the overwhelming influence of epistemologies and ontologies of the Global North on knowledge production and dissemination' (2022: 135), but decolonization efforts can be mistaken for, or confounded with, diversity initiatives and intersectionality theory and praxis. Risam reminds us that these efforts can also obscure the university's ongoing participation in settler colonialism, distract from its aversion to assume responsibility, and deflect from its capacity to bring about meaningful change. One way forward in the recalibration of epistemologies can be illuminated via Rivera Cusicanqui's (2020) notion of *ch'ixi*, as a vehicle for the decolonization of the gestures, acts, and language with which we name the world; as Rivera Cusicanqui has suggested, *ch'ixi* 'expresses the parallel coexistence of multiple cultural differences that do not extinguish but instead antagonize and complement each other' (2020: 66). Such an endeavour is now most commonly expressed through curriculum repair and change.

Usha Iyer's work in film and media studies on what she has called 'a pedagogy of reparations' offers a very sober lesson in the work ahead, stating that there is no simple or straightforward path to repairing or deimperializing university curricula; it is a daunting task with no 'one-time or one-size-fits-all fix, but a continued commitment to constant repair and care' (2022a: 183). More recently in an article entitled, 'Smuggling, infiltrating, usurping', Iyer has presented a more detailed argument for transforming curriculum through 'affective dispositions of joyous usurpation and conspiratorial coalition-building' (2022b). This offers a more joyful lens for engaging in the difficult work ahead, not to mention a way forward that includes collaborative coalition-building that may help assuage the crushing isolation that so many encounter in doing the work. Importantly, more joyful solidarity can be created through attending to informal and under-the-radar decolonial activities such as workshops, film series, and reading groups in lieu of more formal changes to hiring practices or curricular reform. Victoria Bernal (2021: 48) sees this as part of grassroots intellectual endeavours with the potential to prefigure and propel larger-scale changes across the institution. I, myself, have co-organized a reading group dedicated to feminist theory and politics (January 2020–present), and our weekly gatherings over the past several years have been transformational in my own (approach to) work as a university labourer. This open-ended project of reading with others has opened the door to many decolonial musings and activities and has served as the impetus for many current and ongoing collaborations (Assis et al. 2023; Forrest et al. 2024). Such smaller, slower, lower-stakes interventions may very well hold a key to unlocking some vital aspects of our shared collective collaborations. As Iyer makes clear, 'we need a proliferation of demands, manifestos, and countermanifestos that become impossible to ignore' (2022a: 186), if we are to begin building decolonial futures of any import or consequence. Seeing as all of these activities may improve the chances for people to meet, share, commiserate, serve as sounding boards and co-conspirators, there may be more opportunities for decolonial politics to take root via discussion, reading, writing, and creation.

In the above discussion surrounding the potential elements and moves to be made in the articulation of decolonial imaginaries, I have attempted to mark clear distinctions between decolonization and the decolonial. Having foregrounded various writers' and thinkers' approaches to envisioning decolonial futures, I have sought to bring these moves and elements within closer range, so as to inspire greater reflection and action on how already embedded actors might go about engaging in the work of decolonial politics within the university. It would seem that, if any consensus is to be found among the many thinkers invoked in this chapter, it is that they are most sympathetic to paperson's view that we should be more invested in seeing the university operate as a decolonizing institution and not merely to perform the work of decolonizing the university. Without yet fully understanding how to proceed nor yet fully grasping the enormity of the work to be done, I want to end this chapter with the image (or imaginary) of the garden as corresponding reality upon which decolonial futures may be mapped. To do so, Candace Fujikane has already encapsulated what is most promising and generative about this image-imaginary:

> The garden is both an illustration of healing abundance and a metaphor for the relationships people are growing with each other, sharing ancestral knowledge with each other in a way that grows Indigenous economies of abundance beyond the limits of capitalism, occupation, and settler colonialism.
>
> (2021: 166)

Although university workers engaged in decolonial politics may rarely if ever describe their efforts as gardening or garden-work, they may be sowing together different alternatives to capitalism, occupation, and settler colonialism through the act of growing and sharing things with others. What remains to be seen is whether garden work of this kind can be accomplished with, through, or across media, and whether imaginaries-work of any kind will prove to be a crucial force in shifts towards decolonial worlds of the future.

5

Recasting Settler Futures and Advancing Black and Indigenous Futurity

One of the core questions of *Decolonial Media Imaginaries* (DMI) is framed, in part, through my engagement with Candace Fujikane's work in the conclusion of the preceding chapter: can alternatives to capitalism, occupation, and settler colonialism be conceptualized with, through, or across media, and, by extension, can media imaginaries of any kind serve the larger project of bringing decolonial futures into being? To grapple with this question more thoroughly, I now turn to an exploration of contemporary art. With contemporary art museums, galleries, and biennales emerging as lightning rods for reflecting on modern-day institutional practices and politics, as well as burgeoning debates surrounding the need to decolonize these institutions, spaces, and events, the realm of contemporary art offers a useful pivot point for us to consider the decolonial politics currently at play in various locations. In this chapter, I'll survey an Afrofuturist exhibition at the MET, a diasporic exhibition featuring the history and culture of Jamaican Maroons in Nova Scotia, a panhistorical and cosmological Indigenous exhibition at the ROM, the curatorial interventions of an Indonesian art collective at documenta fifteen, and the decolonial handover of SBC Gallery in Montreal/Tiohtià:ke. Together these exhibitions, biennales, and residencies invite settlers and non-Indigenous peoples to glimpse imaginaries that advance Black and Indigenous sovereignty and recast settler futures as not only undesirable but also incompatible with decolonial futures.

Before Yesterday We Could Fly: An Afrofuturist Period Room *(2021–present)*

In November 2021, The Metropolitan Museum of Art (The Met) in New York City celebrated the opening of a highly original exhibition entitled, *Before Yesterday*

We Could Fly: An Afrofuturist Period Room. Exhibition curators chose to harness the convention and aesthetic of the traditional period room to bring to life the lesser-known story of the residents of Seneca Village – 'a vibrant nineteenth century community of predominantly Black landowners and tenants' who, for a very short time, created a flourishing and dynamic settlement in what is now Central Park. Seneca Village's standing as one of New York's first free Black communities was to be short-lived, as the land upon which the community was founded was eventually seized by the city through eminent domain to make way for the creation of what would come to be known as Central Park. With the greenlighting of the park, the city's homeowners and residents were swiftly evicted and displaced, and the village comprised of roughly fifty homes, three churches, two schools, numerous gardens, and several cemeteries was demolished (The Met 2021; Miller 2022). Seneca Village's over thirty-year community history (1825–57) would come to a grinding a halt, and with it, the disappearance of its story and people.

Before Yesterday We Could Fly represents a nuanced, multilayered exhibition designed to centre Seneca Village's story, as well as the lives of its Black community inhabitants. To bring this exhibition into being, The Met invited designer Hannah Beachler and curator Michelle Commander, as well an impressive array of African and African American artists, offering them access to museum artefacts and resources so as to create a much more cohesive and self-reflexive exhibition. Rather than rely solely on historical records and artefacts (of which there are limited traces), the curatorial team conceived of the telling of the story through an Afrofuturist lens: 'Powered by Afrofuturism – a transdisciplinary creative mode that centres Black imagination, excellence, and self-determination – this construction is only one proposition for what might have been, had Seneca Village been allowed to thrive into the present and beyond' (*Before Yesterday*). In many ways, the curators playfully reject the traditional approach to displaying a period room (streamlined aesthetic, coherent display and narrative, fixed historical periodization) and instead opt for an expansive speculative pan-historical reimagining of the past, present, and future of this African and African diasporic community. As Charlene K. Lau remarks in her review of the exhibition, '[*Before Yesterday*] might be cast as an "unperiod" room, for the many cultures, histories and futures of Africa and its diasporas can neither be contained nor reduced to a singular aesthetic or specific moment in time' (2022: 237). The period room is, in effect, a Seneca Village home reimagined as the most suitable space for connecting a speculative past, present, and future of this African diasporic community.

Museum visitors entering this installation will first encounter the structure of a house with raised wooden beams painted white and a number of vantage points from which to observe the home's interiors through windows and an open section that reveals the living room (see Figure 5.1). Perimetre walls surrounding the house feature wallpaper displaying photographic transfers of an 1856 survey map of

FIGURE 5.1: Installation view of *Before Yesterday We Could Fly: An Afrofuturist Period Room*, The Metropolitan Museum of Art, Gallery 508.

Seneca Village, overlaid by portraits of nineteenth-century Black New Yorkers and foliage associated with the okra plant. Each living space represents unique facets of this Afrofuturist revisioning: the kitchen imagines the home's inhabitants to be gardeners, herbalists, and ceramicists; the living room reveals the residents to be champions of technology, visual media, literature, arts and crafts; the hearth and fireplace invoke the importance of meaningfully connecting all of the living spaces into a coherent 'temporal confluence – a merging of past and present into future possibilities' (*Before Yesterday*). Visitors are thus afforded a glimpse of life that was cut short via the destruction of a once-thriving community. In dramatizing this story through museum artefacts and both existing and newly commissioned artworks, the Black imagination is foregrounded to simultaneously resist oppressive histories and to celebrate joyful expressions of Black life and culture.

As a whole, the visual display of colour and vibrancy that animates the home's interiors successfully contributes to the sense of Black joy and pleasure that defines the space. Indeed joy and pleasure appear to be central to the core vision espoused by the curatorial team. As consulting curator Michelle Commander puts it, '[Afrofuturism is] about the liberation of people of African descent. And it's all about the idea of a kind of differing existence from what we're living right now. It's about imagining a place where one can truly be free' (The Met 2021).

In lieu of framing the story of Seneca Village as one of expropriation, displacement, and injustice, *Before Yesterday* presents a much more radical, optimistic, and utopian proposition, by centring a powerful question: what if the inhabitants of this community had been left alone to cultivate their own autonomy and independence? When asked about what she'd hoped a main takeaway from the exhibition would be, lead curator and designer Hannah Beachler unequivocally stated:

> Joy. Black joy. My mission is to teach Black joy before Black pain. No child needs to learn that first. I learned that first. And so, I want people to walk in, and what you see is joyful. What you experience through the pain is joyful. You know, we put hundreds of iron nails in the side of the structure, and they had asked me why, and I said 'Because iron is so important – it is the thing that shackled us and it's the thing that freed us'. I want this to be like that ... I want this, the thing, to be the freedom.
>
> (*Notes from America with Kai Wright* 2023)

The recuperation of the Seneca Village story, coupled with the Afrofuturist reimagining of the community's continued legacy, effectively creates a space for Black liberation to be seen, experienced, and felt. Importantly, while the imaginaries that proliferate via this experiment in other-worlding certainly acknowledge the legacies of slavery and colonialism, they express a unified vision of continuity that sees Black traditions flourish and continue on into a future where Black peoples are free.

In terms of the exhibition display itself, the imagined residents of this home have collected so impressive an array of artefacts, heirlooms, artworks, and general belongings that these objects and things carry the weight of this community's near-total erasure from history (see Figure 5.2). That they are creatively unearthed to reveal a deep reverence for Black (diasporic) culture through references to Harriet Tubman, Zora Neale Hurston, Frederick Douglass, Mae Jemison, Beyoncé, and Stacy Abrams, speaks to the linkages and relations that were potentially denied due to the community's expropriation and displacement. For all its vibrancy, colour, imagination, and attention to detail, the period room could also benefit from the further integration of two key elements: additional historical context and visual descriptions, as well as a more concerted effort to address the historical records and provenance of Met artefacts exhibited in the display. The first element can be explained through The Met's use of multimedia materials to enhance viewers' understanding of the project, most of which appear online and beyond the context of the gallery walls. As a long-term display, the inclusion of these materials can be added over time to attend to different facets of the project's core concerns. The second

FIGURE 5.2: Installation view of the hearth in *Before Yesterday We Could Fly: An Afrofuturist Period Room*, The Metropolitan Museum of Art, Gallery 508.

element requires more institutional engagement on the part of The Met. As Yann Petit notes in his review of the exhibition,

> the visual beauty of the exhibition's pairings and set arrangements overshadowed the controversial and disturbing collecting histories that many of the objects carry with and within them. Ongoing negotiations about the restitution of African artworks put into question the validity of their exhibition at museums when the importance of provenance research was and still is rising.
>
> (2023: 91)

Among the nineteenth- or twentieth-century objects displayed were: a power figure (Nkisi) from the Kongo peoples, a prestige stool from Bamileke or Bamum peoples, a bird staff from the Kingdom of Dahomey, a ceremonial palm wine vessel from the Grassfields chiefdoms of Cameroon, as well as a seventeenth-century crucifix from Angola ('Exhibition objects'). The latter objects could certainly figure in future discussions surrounding provenance and restitution, and whether The Met pursues any of these avenues more concretely is impossible to know.

What we can say is that The Met not only appointed a strong curatorial team capable of steering this project to new heights (who in turn channelled resources and funding to African and African American artists), they also entrusted curators from outside the institution (Beachler and Commander) to repurpose museum artefacts to better reflect the themes and politics embedded in the display (see Figure 5.3). In many ways, this Afrofuturist vision of Seneca Village succeeds in re-centring, in Mitchell and Chaudhury's words, 'Afro-centric cosmologies, histories and epistemes, and [in confronting] ongoing oppressions rooted in anti-Blackness' (2020: 321). The fact that The Met has committed to ensuring *Before Yesterday*'s place as a long-term

FIGURE 5.3: Installation view of the living room in *Before Yesterday We Could Fly: An Afrofuturist Period Room*, The Metropolitan Museum of Art, Gallery 508.

exhibition suggests that the project remains a vital and viable revisionary undertaking. And although sweeping changes to any museum's makeup or governance is rare at best, *Before Yesterday* signals the establishment of a new set of orientations for exhibition work at The Met. The inclusion of a land acknowledgment in the exhibition's visiting guide attempts to foreground and couple together the histories of the Lenape diaspora and the Seneca Village community, in part to acknowledge the oppression endured by these peoples, and in part to celebrate these communities' enduring contributions to the richness of life on this land. And although much has been written on the perceived hollowness and performativity of land acknowledgments as deployed and mobilized by settler institutions (see Stewart-Ambo and Yang 2021), the gesture to amplify historical wrongdoing experienced by Black and Indigenous communities should not be overlooked. The move from acknowledgment to action to freedom and sovereignty for Black and Indigenous peoples must begin to take root in institutions both small and large, and The Met is no exception.

Tyshan Wright: Maroon Town *(2023)*

Since its inception at The Met in 2021, the story of Seneca Village has earned greater visibility in the popular press and within the smaller circuits of artworld publications. The increased visibility surrounding the unjust displacement of a community coupled with the aesthetic reimagining of how a culture might have continued to flourish certainly offers a poignant formula for generating public interest. In 2022, a project touching on stories of the African diaspora, displacement, and (re-)settlement created a similar wave of interest in the Canadian artworld: Tyshan Wright's *Maroon Camp* was shortlisted for the prestigious Sobey Art Award in recognition of the artist's combination of masterful craftwork and gripping pancultural narrative. For *Maroon Camp*, Wright challenges his audience to consider the forced migration of his Maroon ancestors in two times: first, the enslavement and dispersal of his peoples from the Akan region of Ghana to Jamaica (initiated by the Spanish in the seventeenth century), and second, the forced exile of 549 Maroons from Trelawny Town, Jamaica, to Nova Scotia from 1795 to 1796 (perpetuated by the British) (Hollenbach 2023: 50). As an artist who was raised in the mountains of Jamaica – home to the cultural traditions of Jamaican Maroons – and who has forged his artistic practice as a form of preservation of his cultural ancestry – Wright has honed his art through the creation of Maroon instruments, objects, and jewellery. Wright's focus on sacred instruments and ceremonial objects is intentional, in that his Maroon ancestors were forbidden from bringing them on their voyage to Nova Scotia. The power of Wright's work lies in his adaptations (not recreations) of these objects as careful reimaginings of what Maroon culture might have resembled if his ancestors were afforded the freedom to express themselves through their ceremonies and traditions. In the absence of these freedoms and in the scarcity of traditional materials sourced from their Jamaican homelands, Maroons exiled to Nova Scotia would have had to adapt to their new surroundings in the creation of these banned objects. *Maroon Camp* constitutes the reenactment or remodelling of a Maroon camp that features, first and foremost, these forbidden instruments, the significance of which Wright is quick to establish:

> So during the transatlantic slave trade, when our ancestors were brought to the Caribbean, they literally came with nothing physical, you know, nothing tangible. All they came with, really, was their knowledge of survival, so to speak – their connection with nature and sound and vibrations. And so out of the struggle for freedom, they created these sets of instruments.
>
> (cited in Collins 2022)

One of the exhibition's artworks was created during an artist residency at NSCAD University's former Institute for the Study of Canadian Slavery: *Between Slavery and Sovereignty* features a mounted drum comprised of wood, Maroon beads, and deer skin. Tethered to the drum is a chain that connects to two cuffs. Of particular note here is the image of the two open cuffs resting beside the drum, signalling the power of the instrument as a vessel towards freedom and sovereignty. Both the artwork and its title allude to the uneasy tensions experienced by exiled Maroons navigating the hostile environments of the slave-holding society that was Nova Scotia (Nelson 2017). Life in exile would prove untenable for the vast majority of Maroons, bringing about a near-total exodus. As Laura Ritchie recounts: 'After four years of resisting assimilation, protesting working conditions and avoiding conversion to Christianity, almost all of the Maroons left Halifax to resettle in Sierra Leone' (2022: n.pag.). As Wright would have it, these instruments might have offered solace and communion for the Maroons that remained, those who continued to seek greater freedom and autonomy.

The narrative and aesthetic arc of *Maroon Camp* would find even greater expression in a solo exhibition the following year. In 2023, Mount Saint Vincent University Art Gallery would welcome Wright's *Maroon Town* as a continuation of his previous work. The exhibition would feature a staged Maroon town and settlement, a reimagining of Jamaican Maroon life that transgresses fixed historical eras and time periods (see Figure 5.4). Exhibition visitors could be inhabiting a Maroon town in seventeenth-century Jamaica, contemporary Nova Scotia, or somewhere in the future. What is immediately clear is that the exhibition could not dramatize a more hopeful context for confronting the history of Jamaican Maroons. Upon first encountering this work, I, myself, was unfamiliar with this woeful story of African-Jamaican oppression and disenfranchisement. Having organized a visit with students on a day in which Wright was slated to engage in a durational performance (see Figure 5.5), we were all privy to seeing Wright build, in real-time, the structure of

FIGURE 5.4: Installation view of Tyshan Wright: *Maroon Town* at MSVU Art Gallery, Halifax, 23 September 2023 to 9 December 2023. Courtesy of MSVU Art Gallery. Photo by Steve Farmer.

FIGURE 5.5: Durational performance during Tyshan Wright: *Maroon Town* at MSVU Art Gallery, Halifax, 23 September 2023 to 9 December 2023. Courtesy of MSVU Art Gallery. Photo by Steve Farmer.

his Maroon settlement. The process of learning about the brutal hardships experienced by Jamaican Maroons was effectively counterbalanced by the beauty and vibrancy of the exhibition's visual display (curated by Julie Hollenbach). From the outset, the visitor is drawn into the inviting world that is Wright's Maroon town, an environment punctuated by ornately woven crafts, textiles, and instruments, a clothesline and fire pit, a drumming area and video installation, a work of erasure poetry, as well as the structure of the house that is still very much a work-in-progress. Optimism and mourning hang in the balance, as conveyed through a handcrafted skirt adorned with 'red beads representing the lifeblood of the Maroon people and grey beads called teardrops that represent grieving'; the work, entitled *Sarah, after Sarah Colley*, pays homage to those who grieved the departure of their fellow Maroons who'd left for Sierra Leone (Barnard 2023). Grief and optimism punctuate *Hye Won Hye* (meaning 'that which cannot be burned' [Barnard 2023]), in what appears to be the staged aftermath of a fire pit that has all but consumed three drums (two of which are burned and punctured, with a third scarred but intact). Although the destruction of these instruments leaves a visceral charge, the focal point of the artwork is on the instrument that survives (see Figure 5.6). The fire may have extinguished some sacred objects, and may have helped undermine the flourishing

FIGURE 5.6: Installation view of *Hye Won Hye*, Tyshan Wright: *Maroon Town* at MSVU Art Gallery, Halifax, 23 September to 9 December 2023. Courtesy of MSVU Art Gallery. Photo by Steve Farmer.

of Maroon culture, but the tradition, music, and ceremony of Jamaican Maroons have continued in spite of these destructive forces. The fact that these instruments survive so triumphantly in *Maroon Town* reveals a crucial element to Wright's work as an artist. As Julie Hollenbach suggests of Wright's craftwork,

> every single piece of wood, every single bead, every tack and dowel pin, every cut to the skin, every line carved into the wood, every stroke with the sander [...] help sustain a continuum of cultural sovereignty that connects the Maroons to their diasporic roots, and promises branches of thrivance into the future.
>
> (2023: 54)

To witness the actual construction of a dwelling not dissimilar in scope to the housing structure reimagined for Seneca Village has the distinct effect of inviting the visitor to see Maroon culture taking shape before one's very eyes. Surrounded by the imagined ceremonial drums of Wright's ancestors, some of which are concealed as benches to divert attention away from the very colonizers who'd banned their instruments, the space is reimagined as a lively community filled with music and

FIGURE 5.7: Installation view of Tyshan Wright: *Maroon Town* at MSVU Art Gallery, Halifax, 23 September 2023 to 9 December 2023. Courtesy of MSVU Art Gallery. Photo by Steve Farmer.

ceremony (see Figure 5.7). As Elissa Barnard observes, the artist invites all *Maroon Town* visitors to 'sit in front of a home video of Wright outdoors drumming for his children who laugh and play. He invites viewers to sit on and play the drum' (2023: n.pag.). The experience of watching Wright perform on banned ancestral drums to children who at one time would have never experienced freedom on this land, to seeing Wright build a structure as a dwelling for community crystalizes for me the power of decolonial media imaginaries. By engaging past, present, and future, and by extending an invitation to others to participate in the reimagining of life beyond settler colonialism, Wright presents a powerful argument for forms of sovereignty and freedom that involve shared responsibility. The invitation to sit and drum alongside the artist, and to imagine the horizons of his young children's unwritten futures, momentarily reorient us away from the ever-predictable grooves of capitalist and colonial ways of being and into a space of shared reciprocity. In making time to learn about Wright's Jamaican Maroon ancestors, and in paying closer attention to the everyday domestic objects so expertly created by Wright, the visitor comes up against the incompatibility between the historic violence directed towards Maroon peoples and the present and future sovereignty of Maroon descendants. In the act of creating both a Maroon camp and a Maroon town, Wright has pinpointed the exposed nerve ending that is the fallacy of modernity's obsession with progress, and has presented a decolonial counter proposal:

> Something about building this home right here takes me back to a place I've never been […] For the first time I realized how comfortable our ancestors were. You can feel something that brings tears to your eyes, and you realize how happy life was – so simple. We make it so complicated.
>
> (cited in Barnard 2023: n.pag.)

The process of rebuilding life in community in dialogue with one's ancestors, descendants, and ascendants offers a powerful avenue for exploring the potential of decolonial imaginaries.

Kent Monkman: Being Legendary: Confronting Colonialism, Rethinking History *(2022)*

In October 2022, Cree artist Kent Monkman would welcome visitors to the Royal Ontario Museum (ROM) for an astounding exhibition spanning prehistory, the colonial era, and the future. By partnering with the ROM, a natural history and fine arts museum that describes itself as a top ten cultural institution in North America boasting a world-class collection of 18 million artworks, cultural objects, and natural history specimens ('About the museum'), Monkman has worked to advance a different set of understandings regarding the museum as a mythmaking institution. Through this collaboration, Monkman's access to the ROM's vast permanent collection represented an opportunity to reframe how exhibition stories are told and how scientific objects can be repurposed to interface with contemporary artworks to advance knowledge and understanding in relation to historically marginalized Indigenous systems of knowledge. Monkman's *Being Legendary: Confronting Colonialism, Rethinking History* centres Cree worldviews, knowledge, language, and culture and puts them in critical dialogue with Western science and museology in the interests of retelling the history of Turtle Island (Canada/North America) (Forni and Cipolla 2022: 170). As Paulette Steeves (2022: 54) explains as part of the exhibition catalogue, Indigenous people have told origin stories for thousands of years, whereas Western scientists have studied human evolution for only a few hundred years. Monkman draws on this general conceit to tell the story of his shape-shifting alter ego, Miss Chief Eagle Testicle, beginning with her elemental origins in the cosmos ('we are all made of stardust') through her observations surrounding tens of thousands of human generations to the history of colonialism in Canada and beyond. Far from merely relegating

Indigenous experience in Canada to the horrors of the colonial project, Monkman opted to scale back the importance of this narrative through line. As he observed prior to the exhibition's opening: 'I didn't want the colonial project to overtake the conversation. It's part of it, but it's not all of it [...] We don't want to be defined by colonialism' (Mussett 2022: n.pag.). *Being Legendary* thus forges a comprehensive depiction of the world through Cree cosmology, wisdom, and knowledge.

In a playful nod to chronological conceptions of time, Monkman conceives of the timeline of the exhibition's story as beginning in 13.8 billion BCE and continuing to 13.8 billion CE onwards. Through the telling of Miss Chief's origin story as beginning with stardust, the visitor is invited from the outset to think of Indigenous peoples as having inhabited the universe from the very beginnings of creation (see Figure 5.8). Miss Chief's âcimowin – stories that carry Indigenous history and knowledge – begin with the stars and the land, invoking the sacredness of the rock, the mountains, valleys, plains, oceans, lakes, and rivers; and although Miss Chief is careful to centre her story in relation to the Cree peoples, she also invites the audience to see this larger story as their own: 'It is also your story, for

FIGURE 5.8: Installation view of Miss Chief's origin story in Kent Monkman: *Being Legendary at the Royal Ontario Museum*, Toronto, 8 October 2022 to 16 April 2023.

we are all relatives' (Monkman and Gordon 2022: 23). This modest gesture works to create a bridge between exhibition visitors' own sense of time, place, history, and experience with that of the story Miss Chief will tell. To tell this story in vivid detail, Monkman juxtaposes the museum's artefacts and his own artworks to recontextualize our engagement with and understanding of Indigenous knowledge and culture. A horned dinosaur skull is exhibited alongside a Monkman painting that features the mîmîkwîsiwak (the Little People), sacred beings who have protected and honoured the stories embedded in the layers of the Earth's memory (Monkman and Gordon 2022: 38–39). In a companion example, Monkman displays a mammoth tooth (dated between 40,000 and 11,000 years old) next to another painting depicting the mîmîkwîsiwak marvelling at the object amidst an abundance of greenery in nature. As Evan Moffitt posits, ROM artefacts are 'presented in vitrines like scientific evidence of this fairytale history' (2023: n.pag.). By incorporating these artefacts in his artworks – and by juxtaposing these elements in the exhibition space – Monkman brings Indigenous stories to life at the same time that he reanimates the artefact from a Cree perspective little known to museum visitors. And to add even more depth to this curated rewriting of the Western scientific record, Miss Chief is also quick to acknowledge the extinction of beings she'd once known, before expressing her grief exacerbated by the colonial museum's practice of extracting fossils from 'askîy's [the Earth's] embrace to become another commodity for display and trade' (Monkman and Gordon 2022: 38).

Children also occupy a central place in *Being Lengendary*'s narrative arc. Beyond the fascinating depictions of Miss Chief and the Little People sharing space with now-extinct winged creatures and marine animals, Monkman pays special attention to how children were taught everything they needed to live on the land, how to provide sustenance for themselves and their families, and how to live in 'good relation to the Earth and each other' (2022: 15). In *Intermediary Study for Grandmother Knew All the Medicines*, a child is accompanied by her grandmother and Miss Chief in discovering knowledge of plant life for sustenance, healing, and ceremony. Indeed, Monkman's paintings of Cree children and family offer stunning tableaux of communal living on the land, featuring warm colours and smiling faces in vivid detail. In *Constellation of Knowledge*, babies share a similar communal space in the star-filled skies with Indigenous spirits associated with science, medicine, ceremony, art, and laughter. It is only after the settlers come – what Monkman refers to as Colonial Interruption (*c.*1857–2022) – that children's ability to learn from the land is seriously undermined. Through a series of moving and evocative paintings, Monkman depicts the cruelty and brutality of colonialism in Canada. Beginning with the forced removal of children from their families and their subsequent placement in residential schools (referred to as 'forced labour camps') (2022: 90), Miss Chief speaks of the seven generations of suffering that would define this period. The misery, loneliness, and destitution of this moment are distilled in *Study for the Sparrow*, in which a young girl shorn of her hair seeks companionship with a sparrow through a caged window in a bare dormitory adorned with a crucifix. In *Compositional Study for the Going Away Song*, Monkman captures the devastation and helplessness of children forced to witness the unjust hanging of eight Indigenous men at the Battleford Industrial School in 1885. Monkman deepens this sense of loss by exhibiting eight separate pairs of moccasins attributed to unknown Cree and Assiniboine artists. Monkman's purpose is twofold: to invite the visitor to imagine the plight of the people who might have once filled these moccasins, and to call into question the museum's haphazard collection of Indigenous artefacts (the moccasins are described as having been made by 'an artist once known'). As Patrick Quinn (2022) points out, the moccasins are accompanied by eight small paintings representing eight losses experienced by Indigenous communities under colonialism: knowledge, language, medicine, family, ceremony, tradition, hope, and joy (see Figure 5.9).

At this point, the exhibition visitor has now witnessed the depths of Indigenous life and history, as told through the eyes of Miss Chief. Having defused with great empathy the oppressive weight of Canada's history of colonialism as experienced by the Indigenous peoples of Turtle Island, Monkman's final move is to gesture towards a future in which 'our future ancestors light the path to living in miyo pimâtisiwin, living in a good way, with true connection' (Monkman and Gordon

FIGURE 5.9: Installation view of *Study for series* in Kent Monkman: *Being Legendary* at the Royal Ontario Museum, Toronto, 8 October 2022 to 16 April 2023.

2022: 125). Through a series of eleven larger-than-life portraits (see Figure 5.10), Monkman pays homage to Indigenous excellence as a means of conveying that Indigenous communities have not only survived the horrors of colonialism, they also continue to flourish on their own terms. Among those canonized by Monkman, Pauline Shirt (Wandering Spirit School), Teddy Syrette (2Spirit activist), Tasha Beeds (Indigenous grassroots academic), Nick Estes (Red Nation), Briana Olson-Pitawanakwat (Toronto Indigenous Harm Reduction), Gail Maurice (filmmaker), Aurora Ominika-Enosse (social worker), Asinnajaq (artist), Belinda Daniels (nêhiyawak Language Experience), Liz Osawamick (water walker), and Wilfred Buck (star knowledge expert). Each figure is associated with a Cree concept that holds an important place in the articulation of this future ancestry: Maurice embodies miyawâtamowin (the act of celebrating joyfully), Osawamick tâpokêyihtamowin (faith), Beeds kistêyihtamowin (respect), Shirt miyo-pimâtisiwin (the good life), Estes tâpwêwin (truth), and so on (see Monkman and Gordon 2023: 180–96). Together these figures and concepts come to represent the present and future achievements and accomplishments spurred on by Indigenous sovereignty movements. Coming full circle, by the time ROM visitors have reached the end of the exhibit, they will have been afforded the opportunity to inhabit an imaginary so different than anything they will have ever experienced, that their views of the colonial museum and of Indigenous peoples in Canada will be momentarily suspended, if not shifted. In a searching Afterword to the *Being Legendary* catalogue, ROM Director and CEO Josh Basseches (2022: 164) speaks of this exhibition (and of Monkman's work, more specifically) as a collaborative endeavour that was designed to urge the museum to reckon with its colonial history. In a final companion essay, ROM curators Silvia Forni and Craig Cipolla affirm that

FIGURE 5.10: Installation view of portrait series in Kent Monkman: *Being Legendary* at the Royal Ontario Museum, Toronto, 8 October 2022 to 16 April 2023.

Monkman's exhibition makes clear that the violence of both settler and capitalist forms of colonialism 'have no place here' – and that museums have a responsibility 'to engender the construction and presentation of new shared imaginaries' (Forni and Cipolla 2022: 170–71). With *Shame and Prejudice: A Story of Resilience* (2017–20), a blockbuster touring exhibition that centred Canada's genocidal treatment of Indigenous peoples during the colonial era, Monkman foregrounded the strength and resilience of these communities (Bouraly 2019). With *Being Legendary*, Monkman moves well beyond the context of Canadian colonialism to describe, in the words of Miss Chief, a feeling of 'love expanding infinitely into the four directions, all the dimensions, the pastpresentfuture' (Monkman and Gordon 2023: 125). By weaving together Cree stories, knowledge, and history through a vast expanse of time (pastpresentfuture), Monkman solidifies how imaginaries can be mobilized in the recasting of better futures and in the cultivation of miyo-pimâtisiwin (the good life).

ruangrupa: Documenta fifteen (2022)

In February 2019, Jakarta-based artist collective ruangrupa were unanimously appointed as the artistic directors for documenta, one of the most important artworld events in the Western world. This 2022 edition of the event – documenta fifteen – would mark the first time a collective or group of artists from Asia would take the reins as lead curators of the 100-day exhibition. In a distinct move away from embracing the more traditional values associated with art biennales (e.g. beauty, novelty, shock value, contemporaneity), ruangrupa positioned itself from the outset as emphasizing solidarity, collectivism, sustainability, and decolonization as key values to be enacted during their tenure (Mergler 2022: 342). In the press release accompanying the announcement of their appointment, the group took a decidedly different tack in explaining how they would approach their curatorial role: not only would they aim to develop 'a different community-oriented model of resource usage', they would also use their platform to 'focus documenta fifteen on today's injuries, especially ones rooted in colonialism, capitalism, or patriarchal structures, and contrast them with partnership-based models that enable people to have a different view of the world' ('ruangrupa selected'). At the very heart of ruangrupa's curatorial project was the practice of *lumbung*, an expression of shared resource building, equitable distribution, and mutual care ('Glossary'). Of particular note here is how ruangrupa came to situate itself not as guests within the documenta system but as hosts within its own lumbung ecosystem:

> instead of integrating ourselves into the long-established documenta system, we decided to stay on our path. We invited documenta back, asking it to be part of our

> journey. We refuse to be exploited by European institutional agendas that are not ours to begin with.
>
> (ruangrupa 2022: 12)

In rejecting the default mechanisms of cooptation or institutionalization, ruangrupa set out to redraw the lines of possibility within the Eurocentric exhibition context that is documenta.

Their first and most significant contribution to this redrawing of imaginaries was expressed through their horizontal, decentralized, and collectivized approach to curating the event. As Lettau and Canyürek (2024: 8) note, ruangrupa invited fourteen collectives to participate as lumbung members (each of which received a €100,000 budget allocation), who were then offered the opportunity to invite more artists and collectives, which ultimately contributed to the participation of approximately one thousand and five hundred artists at documenta fifteen. This snowball practice of offering access, heightening visibility, and strengthening ties and relations within an artist-led ecosystem was made possible through lumbung processes and practices. The significance of lumbung can also be described as a critical and economic intervention designed to support art and culture in a system that has failed (and continues to fail) its artists. As ruangrupa themselves attested of the lived realities of their invited collaborators, '[m]ost collectives in the lumbung inter-lokal come from the contexts where the state had failed to support the development of infrastructure and a support system for art and culture' (cited in Mergler 2022: 343). The collectivization of artistic participation at documenta ensured that all invited artists/collectives would receive the equivalent of a two-year monthly universal basic income, including an additional equal sum for production costs (Kisić cited in Lettau and Canyürek 2024: 9). In light of these practices of generosity and care, it is no wonder that ruangrupa would coin the following in a slogan-motto-artwork: 'make friends not art' (see Figure 5.11). As documenta unfolded, it became clear that sociality, exchange, and care were inextricably tied to the practice of art-making and to the lived realities of artists' everyday lives. The fruits of collectivism were seen and experienced in public venues such as the Fridericianum (renamed the Fridskul Common Library) through 'cooking together, playing games, conducting workshops, running classes, and organizing childcare' (Juneja and Ziebritzki 2023: 97) – not as productivist demands to create and exhibit artworks (see Figure 5.12). All told, these experiments in collective art-making and living represent a vital antidote to shrinking imaginative horizons, offering a different lens through which to envision surviving an era of interlocking crises.

In addition to fostering collectivity and strengthening relations among the vast networks of artists and groups, ruangrupa was also celebrated for catapulting away from the abstract, modernist, and universalist traditions of documenta towards the

FIGURE 5.11: Poster art by Pangrok Sulap collective artist, Bam Hizal (2022). Courtesy of the artist. Photo credit: Gudkul/Jin Panji.

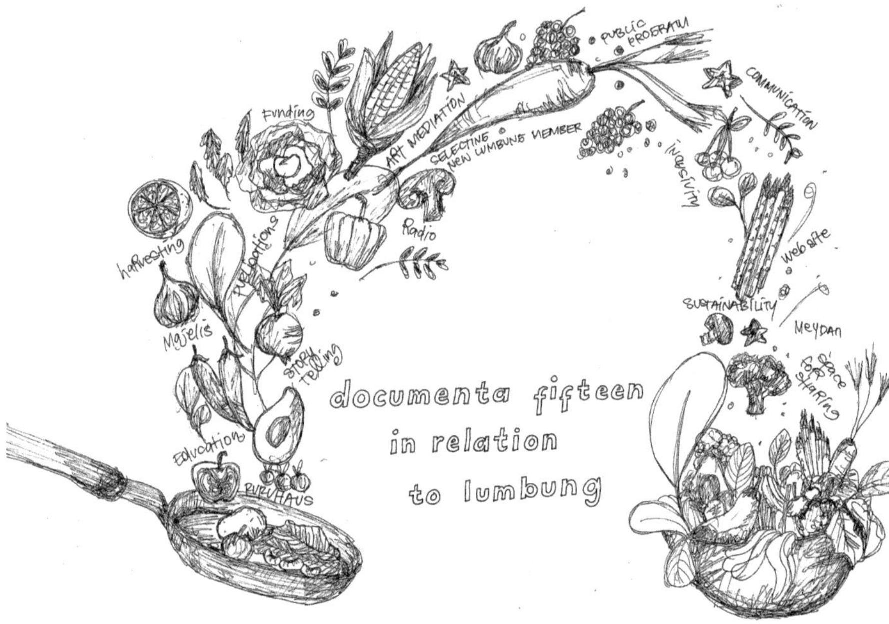

FIGURE 5.12: Artwork by ruangrupa/Daniella Praptono (2022). Courtesy of the artist.

act of teleporting audiences to original locations of participating collectives in the Global South (Kentgen and Cramer 2023: 40). ruangrupa clearly seized the opportunity to foster, in the words of Eric de Bruyn (2023: 66), 'an egalitarian counterpublic sphere' comprised of self-organized artist collectives from the Global South who produce work that reflects their entanglements within decolonial, environmental, and social struggles. With virtually all of the attention being centred on lumbung principles in action, the artworks themselves were accorded far less significance than in more conventional art-market-focused biennales. Despite the shift in focus, German audiences and media remained fixated on the artworks displayed. Within the first days of the exhibition's opening, documenta fifteen had already been cast as antisemitic, anti-Zionist, and anti-Israel. *People's Justice* (2000), a massive banner created by Indonesian art collective Tarin Padi, was deemed antisemitic for its depiction of figures using harmful historical tropes. Add to this some media outlets' concerns regarding the perceived absence of Jewish-Israeli artists, as well as some general outrage over the inclusion of Subversive Film's *Tokyo Reels Film Festival*, a video comprised of pro-Palestinian propaganda from the 1960s to the 1980s (Brown 2022a), and the stage was set to steer discursive talk far away from lumbung and towards the inadmissibility of antisemitic expression in contemporary art and culture. Tarin Padi and ruangrupa immediately accepted responsibility for the mistake and agreed to have the work removed, citing a general blind spot and/or oversight in their understanding of the current German context. For Tarin Padi, the 20-year-old artwork expresses the horrors of the Suharto regime; as they describe in several accounts, they failed to grasp how some of the imagery could be interpreted as antisemitic. The very local context of Tarin Padi's artistic and political environment created the conditions for their artwork to generate a full-blown controversy in the German media public sphere. As they would go on to admit, 'We should have known about this, and that was the mistake [...] We take responsibility for that and we go back to our principles about working together and learning together. Now we work on how to move forward' (Brown 2022b).

Despite sincere efforts to accept responsibility and claim ownership of the mistake, the charge of antisemitism would not only linger for the duration of documenta, it would also overshadow the event as a whole. In their own post-documenta dialogue on the successes and failures of the event, Kentgen and Cramer opine that the lumbung 'everyday experiment in how to actually run a commons' (2023: 90) was sidelined due to the sustained focus on antisemitic imagery – especially in/across German news media. This is, of course, not to say that antisemitic imagery should ever receive a pass of any kind. The point I wish to make is that the expression of decolonial politics from within Euro-Western institutions is seriously fraught. Experiments of the scale and nature espoused by ruangrupa will necessarily create friction, especially within so-called convivial arrangements where one has been invited to bring a unique perspective. The charge of antisemitism would ultimately diminish visibility for and public discussion surrounding the redistribution of resources and infrastructure, the overwhelming representation of artists from the Global South, as well as the epistemological reorientations driven by the presence of ruangrupa and its cascading cadre of collectives. Still, one of ruangrupa's main contributions is to have built 'collective power' (Demos 2023a: 127), collective power that I would argue is capable of engendering new relations and ways of being. Even more to the point, the lumbung model espoused by ruangrupa and their peers at documenta represents a way forward for creating 'decolonial cracks' (Walsh 2023) within dominant institutions. The inherent messiness of producing these cracks is only briefly encapsulated in the example of documenta fifteen, but stories of this kind will only continue to grow as calls for decolonial political action intensify.

Wood Land School: Drawing a Line from January to December *(2017)*

Just as ruangrupa presented a wide-eyed view of how impactful the redistribution of resources and infrastructure could be at one of the world's most important art festivals, so too would the Wood Land School make a powerful statement regarding how small-scale institutions could operate differently in Canada. In 2017, the Wood Land School (WLS) organized by Duane Linklater, Tanya Lukin Linklater, Walter Scott, and cheyanne turions, announced a year-long collaboration with SBC Gallery of Contemporary Art in Montreal. Conceived of as a year-long project, *Wood Land School: Kahatenhstánion tsi na'tetiatere ne Iotohrkó:wa tánon Iotohrha/Drawing Lines from January to December*, WLS began its open-ended endeavour with the following prompt: 'What does it mean for a settler-colonial institution to unknow its power?' In a provisional answer to this question, WLS would call on settler-colonial institutions to offer labour, funds, space, and time to support Indigenous art in the interests of enacting 'mutual accountability, reciprocity, relation across difference and stewardship of resources' (Linklater et al. 2017). For their own part, the host institution (SBC Gallery) would also begin this project with its own set of ontological/existential questions; as then Director/Curator Pip Day has written, 'Can the labor of cultural workers within the ongoing structures of settler colonialism build infrastructures of social change and alternatives to colonial entrenchment on large and small scales?' (2017: 97). To answer this question, SBC agreed to hand over the institutional keys to WLS for the full year: this included oversight of all budgeting and programming decisions, as well as the actual renaming of SBC as Wood Land School. All public traces associated with SBC were removed or made invisible (including the gallery banner and all web content/design) and replaced with Wood Land School materials. SBC's decision to collaborate with WLS on these terms is no small matter: in handing over the keys to a collective seeking to both foreground and advance Indigenous-to-Indigenous relations, agency, and futurity, SBC made itself vulnerable to revealing institutional blind spots and persistent settler colonial power structures, but as Day argues, they did so as a vehicle for 'putting unsettling politics into practice' (2017: 97). This form of institutional reorientation is very much aligned with what Ariese and Wróblewska (2021) would later call 'practicing decoloniality in museums'; indeed, SBC's commitments to this project correspond nicely to at least two of six aims associated with decolonization (as identified by Ariese and Wróblewska): decentring and embracing vulnerability.

On the face of it, one could describe *Wood Land School* as a short-term collaboration that was comprised of three exhibitions and one off-site pedagogical intervention at documenta fourteen, and as a rotating exhibition that featured works by Annie Pootoogook, Billy-Ray Belcourt, Gabrielle L'Hirondelle Hill, Alanis Obomsawin, and Tsēmā Igharas, among others (Rose-Antoinette 2018: 51). To describe this undertaking in this way would certainly highlight WLS's emphasis on centring Indigeneity and Indigenous art as a rebuttal to settler colonial institutions that have historically marginalized and invisibilized Indigenous communities. Curator John Hampton (2017) comes closest to encapsulating the power and promise of *Wood Land School* when he suggests that 'the project is a case study in working through a temporary Indigenous reimagining of an institution – [one that is] unfolding publicly, in real time'. *Wood Land School* would launch during 'Canada 150', the year of Canada's 150-year anniversary of Confederation, in what amounted to a fever pitch of nationwide celebrations devoted to the Canadian nation state (5800 events in total). A national funding program was established for Canada 150 in 2015, a project whose central theme of reconciliation was developed, unironically, without consultation with Indigenous groups ('Mark the 150th'). As Day (2017: 98) recounts, WLS decided on the term 'facilitator' to describe SBC's role in the project, and perhaps most fittingly, Day and her team focused their attention away from the more dominant terms that were circulating – decolonization and reconciliation – towards a more sustained engagement with the notion of unsettling and the labour of care. The fusing together of settler-colonial institutional logics (SBC) and decolonial artistic praxis (WLS), both of which expressed an affinity for privileging Indigenous relations, had the distinct effect of exploring how the recalibration of power relations might assist in furthering Indigenous self-determination (Emmelhainz 2019: 4).

There are moments when an institution may appear to be supporting Indigenous community, but in reality may be undermining the very groups they are meant to uphold. Case in point: the National Gallery of Canada's (NGC) prior handling of international Indigenous art blockbuster exhibition, *Sakahàn* (2013). In a razor-sharp critique of the NGC's installation of the exhibition, WLS collaborator cheyanne turions captures just how easily the settler-colonial institution is able to distance itself from any future reckoning the show might have instigated. Not only was the term 'colonization' noticeably absent from the exhibition's promotional materials, NGC also printed a revealing disclaimer at the visitor entrance to *Sakahàn*: 'The views and opinions expressed in this exhibition are those of the artists and do not reflect the views of the National Gallery of Canada' (turions 2017: 243). As a response to the incompatibility between NGC's disclaimer and *Sakahàn*'s focus on artworks as acts of resistance to and struggles against colonialism and colonization, turions lays bare the hollowness of institutional non-performatives. Taking the NGC to task on numerous fronts, especially with respect to the complex politics associated with institutions engaging in the work of decolonization, turions writes that

> although the NGC cannot grant many of the political demands necessary for Indigenous self-determination, such as the repatriation of lands and resources, it can recognize its own complicity in the settler colonial project and work to materially reconfigure the distribution of aesthetic/cultural power that it traffics in.
>
> (2017: 249)

In the absence of examples of decolonial politics in the realm of large-scale institutions like the NGC, figures like Pip Day have experimented via small-scale organizations like SBC to partner with collectives such as Wood Land School to put into motion the material, aesthetic, and cultural reconfigurations necessary to carry out a decolonial agenda. For Jonah Gray, the result is the creation of a new model that celebrates 'Indigenous-initiated quasi-institutions that propose alternate, anti-colonial, sovereign spaces that are comfortable moving between the museum and the bush' (2017: 16). The tension between the institution and the land occupied a central place in the Wood Land School's decolonial approach to reimagining SBC. For Ronald Rose-Antoinette (2018: 53), this exhibition asks its audience to refuse the aesthetic platitudes of the gallery in favour of the 'artfulness of the land'; more pointedly, he asks: instead of collapsing everything into the realm of private property and ownership, how might endeavours of this kind incite visitors to become 'practitioners of the land?' On one level, the WLS's takeover of SBC has now produced the conditions for onlookers to imagine how small-scale (and arguably large-scale) arts and culture organizations could go about meaningfully intervening as agents of decolonial politics; on another level, the WLS-SBC collaboration offered a very grounded (and grounding) example of how 'systemic institutional white settler supremacy can be uprooted in favour of Indigenous ways of thinking, doing, and being' (Decter and Taunton 2022: 98). Not to be outdone, Eléa Regembal (2017) has added an additional facet of this project to consider: that Wood Land School has succeeded in interpellating settlers to educate themselves, assume responsibility, and take the necessary steps needed to participate in the long process of decolonization ahead. The combination of institutional oversight and artistic inclusion specifically created in the interests of furthering Indigenous agency and futurity has made possible new lines of flight for engaging in decolonial politics.

Nearing the end of the *WLS* exhibition year, members of the collective were already ruminating publicly on the impacts a project of this kind might have more broadly. WLS founder Duane Linklater was quite candid in his view that the SBC collaboration was only made possible because the organization was 'willing to unknow the power they yield' (cited in Carney 2017: n.pag.). And despite the collective's relative enthusiasm for collaborations of this kind, they were quick to note that they were already bracing themselves to be invited back to collaborate with institutions that continue to reproduce well-worn colonial and artworld power relations. During the same interview, turions went so far as to claim that the project shouldn't be adopted as a model for other institutions engaging in the work of decolonization. Tanya Lukin Linklater also stressed that despite their calls for widespread institutional change, they remained particularly invested in fostering Indigenous-to-Indigenous relations. In bringing together a variety of perspectives on the experiment that was the *Wood Land School*, I've attempted to highlight how infrastructure, representation, and relations all form a crucial component in the expression of Indigenous art on Turtle Island. Small-scale experiments of this kind point the way towards decolonial futures in/across settler colonial institutions that may or may not be willing or ready to engage in this work.

Conclusion

I began this chapter with a question surrounding the promise of and potential for media to produce alternatives to capitalism and settler colonialism. I also posed a companion question regarding the viability of whether media imaginaries could more concretely contribute to bringing decolonial futures into being. To answer these questions, I've taken a more indirect route by exploring media as conceptualized as a binding intermediary presence in the practice, instituting, and institutionalization of contemporary art. Through the five examples discussed above, I've paid close attention to the internal and outward dynamics expressed through collaborations fostered between artists and institutions. In doing so, I've attempted to tease out the ways in which Black and Indigenous forms of sovereignty are reimagined in such a way as to recast individual, collective, and institutional settler futures as both undesirable and at odds with decolonial futures. In highlighting these small- and large-scale collaborations, I make the larger point that the expression of decolonial politics is always fraught in the realm of media, arts, and culture, even when host institutions are decidedly supportive of the work they have signed on to exhibit. The enormous reserve of time, resources, energy, labour, care, and solidarity needed to begin this work is clear through each set of examples surveyed in this chapter. To continue this decolonial work in and through cultural institutions requires deep commitments on the part of artists and extensive reorientations on the part of institutions. Given the unevenness and unpredictability these collaborations can create, it is impossible to gauge what kinds of experiments will yield the most fruitful outcomes. One promising aspect associated with these ever-increasing collaborations is that they have the capacity to simultaneously weaken, if not dissolve, the hegemonic standing of settler imaginaries all the while presenting astounding new visions for Black and Indigenous decolonial futures yet unwritten.

6

The Decolonial Imaginaries-Work of Indigenous Futurisms

In the previous chapter, I explore the work of decolonial media imaginaries as they are mobilized from within the context of museums, galleries, and artworld institutions. By drawing closer attention to collaborations between artists and institutions, I've shown one facet of the constraints and possibilities that are currently defining the decolonial politics at play within the realm of contemporary art. In this chapter, I examine the imaginaries-work so central to the realm of Indigenous art, as a means of further advancing discussions surrounding Indigenous sovereignty, resistance, and most notably, futurity. By specifically engaging the work of Indigenous futurist art, and of future-oriented internet media projects produced in Turtle Island, I will shed greater light on how media imaginaries of this kind may come to enact meaningful decolonial politics. In what follows, I present careful readings of Skawennati's machinima series, *TimeTraveller*™, Lisa Jackson's virtual reality installation, *Biidaaban: First Light*, and Jennifer Wemigwans' Indigenous knowledge website, FourDirectionsTeachings.com. For Skawennati, Jackson, and Wemigwans, the work they produce is deeply invested in cultivating imaginaries that draw from past, present, and future, so as to ensure that Indigenous histories, language, knowledge, culture, and imagination not only survive but thrive into the future. With a focus on companion media platforms and genres – video simulations, virtual reality, multimedia websites – this chapter addresses some of the media dynamics and technological affordances harnessed by each artist that offer increased opportunities for the creation of new imaginaries-work to take root. Inspired by the visions and imaginaries put forward by all three artists, I extrapolate from these art-based interventions (e.g. Loveless 2019; Pérez 2019) as exemplars of 'the kinds of genre-busting and fearless experimentation needed for constructing decolonial futures' (Bernal 2021: 51). The imaginaries-work presented through these examples offers a powerful glimpse of how decolonial politics are being mobilized across Turtle Island in the interests of advancing Indigenous sovereignty and futurity.

Replacing settler colonial paradigms with Indigenous-led futurist imaginaries

Before turning to these artists' endeavours, it will be useful to contextualize how their work might best be situated through the lens of Indigenous Futurisms, and how this conceptual paradigm helps us to better appreciate a kind of decolonial ethos. In recent years, Indigenous Futurisms has garnered growing attention for its fusion of creativity, decolonizing critique, and hope (Stewart 2023: 292). Grace Dillon is first credited with conceptualizing and popularizing the term through her work as the editor of *Walking the Clouds: An Anthology of Indigenous Science Fiction* (2012). Dillon writes that the works of Indigenous science fiction that populate *Walking the Clouds* are representative of a distinctive spirit that resonates through the concept: 'Indigenous Futurisms are not the product of a victimized people's wishful amelioration of their past, but instead a continuation of a spiritual and cultural path that remains unbroken by genocide and war' (2016: 2). Central to Dillon's formulation of the term is the power ascribed to art in the continuation of Indigenous flourishing that both precedes and supersedes colonial histories. Literary explorations in *Walking the Clouds* take the form of multiple sub-genres, including Contact, Indigenous science and sustainability, and Native apocalypse, among others. Art under the guise of Indigenous science fiction offers artists a vital framework for producing 'new ways of reading our ancient natures' (Dillon 2016: 6). As Dillon would argue, such new readings of ancient natures also produce an undeniable reconceptualization of time as 'pasts, presents, and futures that flow together like currents in a navigable stream' (2012: 3).

Such visions of Indigenous futurity are nowhere present in the settler imaginaries depicted in most popular future-oriented genres such as science fiction literature; indeed, these works have a tendency to reproduce and even deepen imperial and colonial prejudices and biases at the expense of Indigenous communities (Lewis 2016: 37). One rebuttal to the damaging colonial overtures at work in the realm of art is boldly articulated by Bronwyn Carlson, who states that 'settler futures are astonishingly myopic' (2023: 16). As a champion of Indigenous futurist work, Carlson asks us to imagine a paradigm shift that involves settlers recognizing the hollowness of their prevailing logics of possession and domination, and of seeing Indigenous peoples as peoples of the future (2023: 16). Skawennati takes this challenge one step further by asserting that if Indigenous peoples can't imagine themselves in the future, there is a strong possibility that they simply won't be there (cited in Sandals 2016). Thus, a core element of replacing settler colonial paradigms with Indigenous-led futurist imaginaries is tied to expressions of Indigenous sovereignty spurred by a process of 'imagining and enacting a future for Indigenous peoples – a future based on terms of their own making' (Smith cited in Arvin et al. 2013: 24).

The future is often distilled through a colonial lens, deployed in the interests of shoring up settler-colonial power structures, and articulated through the ever-ubiquitous trope of Indigenous peoples as always disappearing and/or vanishing (Arvin 2015; Furtado 2024). The future can also exist 'beyond the imaginative and territorial bounds of colonialism' – as made palpable through the decolonial aesthetics of Indigenous art, in what amounts to a rich and varied ensemble of practices that weave together 'past and future Indigenous worlds into new currents of present struggle' (Martineau and Ritskes 2014: IV, X). At stake is the broader project of creating speculative futures capable of 'subverting the death imaginary ascribed to Indigenous bodies within settler colonial discourse' (Nixon 2020: 332) and of replacing these tropes with visions of Indigenous futures situated seven generations ahead (Lewis 2016: 37). For multimedia artists such as Elizabeth LaPensée, Indigenous Futurisms are rooted in what she calls 'the hyperpresent now', a moment that takes seriously the notion that Indigenous peoples 'look seven generations before, and seven generations ahead' (cited in Fricke 2019: 119). This navigable stream of time spanning (past- and future-oriented) seven generations offers a key to unlocking what Tanya Lukin Linklater refers to as 'desirous kinds of Indigenous futurity', that is, 'the re-emergence of Indigenous knowledges and epistemologies through repatriation of our lands and re-centring of our cultural selves' (2017: 149). In terms of contextualizing the impact for artists creating imagined Indigenous futures, the act of creation is an opportunity 'to look beyond the injustices of the past and the struggles of the present, to an expansive, hopeful, and vibrant future' (Lewis 2016: 49). The primary vehicle for enacting these pasts-presents-futures is the story via highly adaptive forms of storytelling. As Leanne Betasamosake Simpson argues in *A Short History of the Blockade*, 'stories not only fill our worlds, they make our worlds' (2021: 6). As she sees it, storytelling is as much about telling stories and building worlds as it is about living in and inhabiting these worlds. For Indigenous artists to harness the power of imagination, narrative, media, technology, and tradition in the service of Indigenous futurity is to advance the interlocking projects of decolonization and Indigenous sovereignty. I now turn to a broader discussion of Skawennati, Jackson, and Wemigwans to more clearly distil the ways in which Indigenous art is redrawing the contours of decolonial politics through an impressive array of decolonial imaginaries.

Decolonial media imaginaries and Indigenous futures in Skawennati's TimeTraveller™

July 2024 would mark my first time visiting www.TimeTravellerTM.com, a website that invites internet users to immerse themselves in Indigenous history via a futuristic gaming system. Users gain access to the platform via TimeTraveller™ glasses that create 3D environments based on user search queries. The glasses are equipped with a Heads-up Display (HUD) offering maps, real-time translation, and a 'Find-A-Date Search Engine' capable of immersing users in historical experiences, such as pivotal events for Indigenous communities of Turtle Island (see Figure 6.1). One quickly realizes that the website is less a portal for virtual reality game playing on the part of users than it is a web series comprised of nine machinima episodes that centre Indigenous experience through the reimagining of events ranging from the Dakota Sioux Uprising (1862) to the occupation of Alcatraz Island (1969) and the Oka Crisis (1990).

Indeed, *TimeTraveller*™ was created by Mohawk artist Skawennati and conceived of via virtual gaming platform Second Life. The series follows the time-travelling adventures of Hunter, a young Mohawk man living in Montreal in a twenty-second century (c. 2121) culture dominated by consumerism, technology, and overpopulation. During his 3D time travel experiences, he encounters Karahkwenhawi, a young twenty-first century (c. 2011) Mohawk woman from Kahnawake, with whom he will eventually share his adventures. In Episode 1 (EP01), Hunter describes himself as part of a lineage of Mohawk survivors, and as a highly skilled Indigenous person whose greatest assets seem oddly out of place in the twenty-second century. Hunter's travels begin at home in his apartment when he is interpellated by an advertisement for TimeTraveller™, a provocation that inspires him to visit with his ancestors and reconnect with his role models (Hunter's words), with the more general idea that these travels will do him some good. The series thus begins in the future with an eye towards deepening the connections among ancestral histories, the present, and the future of Indigenous peoples. In reflecting on core elements of her work,

FIGURE 6.1: *Find-A-Date*™ *Search Engine* HUD (Heads-up Display) from Skawennati's *TimeTraveller*™ website, https://www.timetravellertm.com/about.html.

Skawennati emphasizes the significance of future-oriented artworks depicting the lives and trajectories of First Nations communities: 'My work is about imagining Indigenous people in the future. We need to imagine the future of our nations, because we have been relegated to the past for far too long' (cited in Allaire 2020). In nine compact episodes, Skawennati invites her audience to witness history from an Indigenous perspective that privileges the whims, curiosities, and desires of her protagonists as they (re)discover the stories and experiences of their ancestors. Or, as Hunter suggests prior to the conclusion of Episode 1, 'If there's one thing every Indian knows, it's this: when it comes to history, always get a second opinion'. Such a pronouncement serves to prepare the audience to revisit colonial histories and encounters from within an anticolonial framework.

TimeTraveller begins with Hunter's immersion into Indigenous life and culture through virtual visits to Acton Township, MN (1862), Kanehsatake (Oka), QC (1990), and Alcatraz Island, CA (1969). Through these 'immersions', Hunter experiences the starvation and injustices befallen the Dakota Sioux, adding touches of empathy and compassion surrounding their mistreatment at the hands of the US Government. Hunter's time with the Mohawk people of Kanehsatake during the Oka Crisis is especially formative: 'I learned a lot about my [Mohawk] culture. It was like summer school behind the barricades' (EP03). During this visit (an experience equivalent to several weeks of gameplaying), Hunter would come to decipher a crucial distinction: that his ancestors had no interest in being or becoming Canadian citizens because they were 'already citizens of the Iroquois Confederacy'. During his equally lengthy time spent on Alcatraz, Hunter witnesses young charismatic Mohawk Richard Oakes' richly ironic proclamation that would spearhead an 18-month occupation of the island (Treuer 2019): 'We, the native Americans, re-claim the land known as Alcatraz Island in the name of all American Indians by right of discovery' (The Proclamation—Alcatraz Occupation 1969 n.d.). Both visits to Kanehsatake and Alcatraz crystallize for Hunter the significance of Indigenous sovereignty and self-determination.

In an interesting progression of events, Hunter moves from the distant past in Episodes 1–3 to his more recent past in Episode 4, as seen in a live broadcast from Winnipeg Olympic Stadium in the year 2112 (see Figure 6.2). All eyes are glued to the event's host via jumbotron screen, an Indigenous male celebrity who offers the crowd an overview of things to come: some of the 'best drumming and dancing in the galaxy', a punk concert, and a fashion show. According to our host, Indigenous culture has been experiencing a full-blown resurgence. The audience learns that although Indigenous gatherings such as powwows were once outlawed, the twenty-first century would tell a far different story: record numbers of Indigenous babies were born, powwows grew in capacity to showcase more dancers, singers, drummers, encompassing bigger shows, larger audiences, and securing worldwide broadcasting rights (EP04). For the series' twenty-first-century protagonist,

FIGURE 6.2: Skawennati, *Jingle Dancers Assembled*, 2011, machinimagraph from *TimeTraveller*™, 16:9.

Karahkwenhawi, to attend the Winnipeg stadium event is to catch a glimpse of a future in which Indigenous peoples are thriving. The visual imprint of seeing a stadium full of Indigenous peoples participate in a full-blown celebration of art, culture, and ceremony represents one of Skawennati's main motivations embedded across *TimeTraveller*™: to create a powerful imaginary of Indigenous futures punctuated by Indigenous resurgence, sovereignty, and freedom. The power of this imaginary comes to life through both Hunter and Karahkwenhawi's time travel experiences. Accessing the future is very much tied to their willingness to visit and experience first-hand the lives and events associated with historical figures such as Kateri Tekakwitha, Pocahontas, Sacagawea, and Richard Oakes. Although the gaming system offers two gameplayer modes – Fly-on-the-Wall (passive) and Intelligent Agent (active) – both protagonists ultimately harness Intelligent Agent mode to express their agency during their travels. Intelligent Agent mode does not enable users to change the course of history, but it does offer them additional leeway to deepen their learning and understanding of these often poorly understood historical moments, figures, and phenomena. For example, Karahkwenhawi not only learns more about Kateri Tekakwitha (1680) by forging an intimate friendship with her, she is also able to experience 'a living breathing longhouse in all its glory' through their interactions together. Such distinct aspects of her time travel enrich her overall experience and prompt her to reexamine everything she believed to have known about Tekakwitha (see Figure 6.3).

FIGURE 6.3: Skawennati, *Karahkwenhawi Relaxing*, 2010, machinimagraph from *TimeTraveller*™, 16:9.

Such forays in the reimagined past inspire our protagonists to extend their conceptions of time, so much so that they decide to visit Tenochtitlan in the year 1490 (Aztec Empire). In offering a rationale for the trip, Karahkwenhawi quips: 'I like the idea of going somewhere pre-contact, before Columbus or Cortez got here. It's like a vacation from colonialism' (EP07). This idea of distancing themselves from colonialism will eventually lead Karahkwenhawi and Hunter to decide on living in the future together. For Karahkwenhawi, an art history university student, the opportunity to attend an exhibition dedicated to 'Early 21st Century Indigenous Art' would inspire an epiphany: 'I knew I was where and when I was supposed to be' – the Indigenous future (see Figure 6.4). The final two episodes track the couple making multiple visits between the years 2011 and 2121, with Karahkwenhawi proclaiming in the end that 'the best stuff is the future' (EP09). She reveals that the Cree separate from Quebec in 2051 to form a confederacy with their First Nations cousins to the west, with the Haudenosaunee, Anishinaabe, and Blackfoot to follow suit. Due in part to his dedicated and imaginative gameplay, Hunter ends up winning a TimeTraveller contest that earns him $1 trillion and an invitation to host the platform's newest reality show: *Extreme Time Travellers*. Skawennati's *TimeTraveller*™ ends with a lavish viewing party to launch the first episode of the new reality show, which ends up being the first episode of Skawennati's machinima series. The underlying conceit, of course, is that Hunter and Karahkwenhawi's critical encounters with colonial history will now gain a

FIGURE 6.4: Skawennati, *Epiphany (featuring a digital representation of 'cloudscape', an installation by Hannah Claus)*, 2013, machinimagraph from *TimeTraveller*™, 16:9.

sizeable audience via the platform, which will further assist in deepening knowledge and understanding of Indigenous history and culture; images and imaginaries tied to Indigenous resurgence and sovereignty will also assume an important place in the series. In a 2015 talk entitled, 'Imagining the next seven generations', Skawennati identifies a major problem that has lingered far too long: a scarcity of images representing Indigenous peoples in the future. Throughout her career, her approach to remedying the problem has been to create art in cyberspace, of which *TimeTraveller*™ represents but one example. As Skawennati sees it, imaginaries that capture the vitality, beauty, resilience, vibrancy, and solidarity of Indigenous peoples are crucial to enhancing Indigenous life in the present, and of improving relations between settlers and First Nations communities. Multimedia projects like *TimeTraveller*™ offer prescient glimpses into the future through decolonial media imaginaries that foreground the depth and breadth of Indigenous storytelling.

Land, language, and light in Lisa Jackson's Biidaaban: First Light

TimeTraveller™ is set in the year 2121, just shy of a century into the future. The next Indigenous futurist project to be discussed assumes a similar posture, positing what the future will look like under the purview of Indigenous artists deploying virtual reality. As mentioned in the previous chapter, 2017 marked the beginning of 'Canada 150' – Canada's 150-year anniversary of Confederation. Just as many of the proposed events were tailored in the interests of celebrating the history of the Canadian nation state, some projects would pivot decisively away from celebratory versions of this history to articulate something quite different. For *2167*, a virtual reality (VR) project launched by imagineNATIVE, TIFF, Pinnguaq, and the Initiative for Indigenous Futures, 'Canada 150' audiences would be offered a glimpse 150 years into the future through an Indigenous lens (Skura 2016). Six projects were commissioned in 2016 to be screened the following year at either the TIFF or imagineNATIVE festivals. The conceit of bypassing 'Canada 150' celebrations altogether in favour of a virtual exploration of Indigenous art and imagination in the next 150 years constitutes a clear expression of Indigenous Futurisms. The choice of VR was both deliberate and unanimous for this project. Responding directly to the promise of delivering an Indigenous-led VR experience within the context of 'Canada 150', then head of TIFF Cinemateque, Jesse Wente, spoke to some of the challenges and opportunities therein: 'It would be great for Canadians, especially non-Indigenous Canadians, to spend a moment imagining an Indigenous future, and not one you can see mediated by rows of seats in 2-D. Canadians are very disconnected from Indigenous people' (quoted in McGinn 2017). Jason Ryle, artistic director at imagineNATIVE and one of the chief architects behind *2167*, likens VR as a medium that may come closest to channelling Indigenous modes of oral storytelling, specifically through its capacity to offer point of view, as well as a sense of space and environment (Johnson 2017). VR was also selected for its propensity to produce visceral experiences, an element that could instigate audiences to connect more deeply with Indigenous stories of the future (Everett-Green 2018). The power of the medium was celebrated among many of *2167*'s attendees and critics, among them journalists like Lucius Dechausay (2018) who stated that projects of this kind are more than a mere exercise in technical and aesthetic prowess – 'it's about a future where Indigenous values, language, and land are all integral to survival'. The overriding project theme and platform would ultimately set the tone for invited artists to pursue creative and dynamic collaborative art pieces. Among them, storylines depicting automated police surveillance orbs interrupting a father and son goose hunt on sovereign Mohawk territory (Danis Goulet's *The Hunt*), a young boy travelling through a wormhole back to his ancestral territory (Scott Benesiinaabandan's *Blueberry Pie Under a Martian Sky*), and a disorienting visit to Los Alamos, NM, where it is difficult to decipher whether the enflamed craters and mountains are tied to the destruction of the environment or to its restoration (Postcommodity's *Each Branch Determined*).

One of the most impactful projects associated with *2167* has been described as a world in which 'nature has reclaimed the city – and imperiled languages have been reborn' (Balkissoon 2018: n.pag.). Anishinaabe artist Lisa Jackson's *Biidaaban: First Light* is set in the future city of Toronto, which has escaped both settler colonial and capitalist paradigms. When Bronwyn Carlson (2023: 21) poses a question central to the politics of Indigenous Futurisms – 'what can a future look like that is free of settler colonialism and free of oppression?' – one might readily point to *Biidaaban* as a useful example. According to Jackson's harmonious vision of a reconciled and reclaimed Tkaronto (Toronto), all species live in relation 'rather than humans living at the top of a pyramid' (cited in Hardawar 2018: n.pag.). Set in downtown Toronto's Nathan Philips Square (the current seat of political power and civic governance), the city is recast as both lush and overgrown, as well as dilapidated and abandoned (see Figure 6.5). The hollowness of ubiquitous advertising and the oppressive constancy of industrial pollution have been replaced with the serenity of the natural world punctuated by the sounds of crickets, frogs, birds, leaves, and waterways. Jackson's team had surely deliberated on how to create spaces for reflection on, and comparisons between, the contemporary moment that was 2017 and their imagined urban future when they selected Nathan Philips Square as one of the dedicated sites for experiencing the installation. One can only imagine the jarring disconnect between shifting from a present-day Toronto (large crowds, urban soundscapes, visual and environmental pollution) to a future Toronto overgrown with greenery, free of electricity and power grids, and dominated by species other than human beings. Mathew Borrett, one of the project's lead 3D/VR designers,

FIGURE 6.5: Mathew Borrett, *Hypnagogic City*, 2017. Courtesy of the artist.

describes the built environment of *Biidaaban* as 'more about many small events over a long period of time' (Knight 2018: n.pag.); likening the imagined changes of the year 2167 to what author Alan Weisman recounts in his 2007 non-fiction book, *The World without Us*, Borrett sees *Biidaaban* as an exploration of what would transpire across the planetary ecological balance if technology and people no longer existed. Whatever transpires between 2017 and 2167 is less important than what is depicted in the Toronto of the future. What's clear for Jackson is that 'the Indigenous roots of this place continue even here, in the city centre' (cited in Everett-Green 2018: n.pag.).

The project's official synopsis (courtesy of project partner, the National Film Board of Canada) is instructive, as it fills in some of the details I have yet to cover:

> Toronto's Nathan Phillips Square is flooded. Its infrastructure has merged with the local fauna; mature trees grow through cracks in the sidewalks and vines cover south-facing walls. People commute via canoe and grow vegetables on skyscraper roofs. Urban life is thriving.
>
> (Media Space 2018)

Rounding out the scene, buildings are covered with moss, tobacco leaves can be seen drying on a rack, and a tent consisting of translucent hide occupies our field of vision (Everett-Green 2018). One refreshing aspect of this project is the outright rejection of a dystopian narrative; instead, we witness a celebration of nature within the urban context of what was a major metropolitan city. More than this, *Biidaaban*'s depiction of a flourishing urban life beyond colonialism and capitalism creates room for the representations of Indigenous culture to take hold via allusions to Sky Woman and Grandmother Moon (Rattan 2018). The restoration of balance in nature figures as prominently a theme as does the resurgence of Indigenous languages. *Biidaaban* centres the traditional languages of the territory – Wendat (Huron), Kanien'kehá:ka (Mohawk), and Anishinaabe (Ojibway) – as a means of exploring 'how Indigenous languages can provide a framework for understanding the [VR] user's place in the world and open up a space for new imaginings of the future' ('MIT Docubase'). Indeed, Jackson and her team make excellent use of VR to create explicit ties between land and language. Each language is incorporated into all three of the installation's built environments: a lower-level introduction to a flooded subway platform, a ground-level view of Nathan Philips Square (see Figure 6.6), and a starry sky view of the square from a nearby rooftop (see Figure 6.7). The result being that VR users are encouraged to see land and language as inextricably linked, and that language represents an essential facet of understanding these ancestral lands. As Jackson notes of her Tkaronto of 2167, 'languages that have been spoken here for many thousands

FIGURE 6.6: Still from *Biidaaban: First Light*. Image used with the permission of the National Film Board of Canada.

FIGURE 6.7: Still from *Biidaaban: First Light*. Image used with the permission of the National Film Board of Canada.

of years grow back in the same way as the plant life and the other things that are native to this world' (cited in Wilson 2019: n.pag.).

One strategy used to clarify the relation between land and language comes through the incorporation of the Haudenosaunee Thanksgiving Address, for which Jackson received permission to include from members of the Six Nations (Rattan 2018: n.pag.). The viewer observes the text being displayed and recited in the three languages (later dissolved into translated English): 'We give thanks and acknowledge her, our mother the Earth that supports our feet. All our minds are one' (Dechausay 2018: n.pag.). The experience of hearing this expression of thanks in traditional Indigenous languages through VR produces a sense of reciprocity and harmony in one's relation to the natural environment and even enhances one's sense of the relay between land, language, and relations. On this point, Jackson insists that the inclusion of both Indigenous and English text serves to first ground, then immerse, the user as they navigate a radically transformed city: 'The way we did it, it's not just subtitles, it really becomes almost part of the environment that is active and actually engaged with you, you sort of feel connected to it' (cited in Kabatay 2019: n.pag.). During this eight-minute installation, viewers travel to a future urban landscape where the vestiges of colonialism and capitalism are subdued and where the celebration of the natural world is tied to the wonderment of experiencing Indigenous languages in full bloom. Although Indigenous languages on Turtle Island have long been protected and maintained under even the harshest colonial conditions, their broader revitalization has remained slow and hard-won. As Denise Balkissoon (2018) reported at the time of the installation, all 60 Indigenous languages in Canada are relatively fragile: by way of example, only approximately three thousand five hundred people still know Kanien'kehá:ka (Mohawk), as little as 100 Wolastoq speakers remain, and Cree vocabulary has decreased from roughly 600,000 words to 15,000. *Biidaaban*'s vibrancy comes from its clear-eyed deployment of Indigenous Futurisms as a springboard for depicting Indigenous resurgence as realized through the reclamation of land and the revitalization of language. To experience the wonder of seeing stars cascade from all directions under a giant moon in any context would be difficult not to appreciate. Biidaaban is the Anishinaabemowin word for the first light of dawn, a moment of the day that invokes that anything is possible; the word is also said to refer to the notion of the past and future converging on to the present (Johnson 2018: n.pag.). As *Biidaaban* has shown, these aesthetic, cosmological, and temporal confluences are at the heart of the Indigenous futurist project – and these first-light-of-dawn imaginaries are all within reach.

Constellations of Indigenous knowledge in Jennifer Wemigwans' FourDirectionsTeachings.com

Indigenous languages occupy a central place in *Biidaaban* because they embody the essence of Indigenous life and culture. Part of Jackson's concerns expressed in *Biidaaban* and in a recent broader-scale companion project (*Transmissions*) are tied to the threat of these languages' demise:

> We know that these languages continue to be threatened. What I am particularly concerned with is what is contained within them. The ideas within these languages are incredibly crucial right now, particularly in the times we're in as it regards the environment.
>
> (cited in Smith 2019: n.pag.)

In depicting futures in which Indigenous languages are flourishing, Jackson suffuses her art with imaginaries that produce rebuttals to the fatalism associated with pronouncing the inevitable extinction of these languages. In Jackson's register, the future informs the present as to the role language revitalization may play in the decades and centuries to come. In the final media project to be discussed, I examine the imaginaries-work of Annishnaabekwe scholar and producer Jennifer Wemigwans through FourDirectionsTeachings.com (FDT), a website dedicated to Indigenous knowledge and philosophy (see Figure 6.8). Launched in 2006 by Wemigwans and her production team at Invert Media, the project was conceived in the interests of protecting and promoting Indigenous knowledge online (Wemigwans 2018). FDT offers visitors the opportunity to experience teachings from Indigenous Elders and Knowledge Keepers from among five of the original First Nations across Turtle Island: Blackfoot, Cree, Ojibwe, Mohawk, and Mi'kmaq. Responding to a sense of urgency on the part of Knowledge Keepers to simultaneously protect and share this knowledge more broadly for the benefit of Indigenous communities (Sharma and Wemigwans 2022: 223), Wemigwans' work holds an important place in the creation of new horizons and imaginaries for the transmission and preservation of Indigenous culture.

As Wemigwans makes clear in *A Digital Bundle* (2018), a book-length exploration of this project, FDT represents a substantive contribution to the proliferation of and visibility for Indigenous knowledge on the internet. As she puts it, for Indigenous peoples to be present on the internet constitutes an act of resistance to ongoing colonization efforts, as well as a rejection of the colonial view that Indigenous peoples do not exist (2018: 29). Wemigwans and her team disavow this notion of the disappearing Indian (King 2012) and/or the invisibilization of the first peoples of Turtle Island through the creation of a website designed

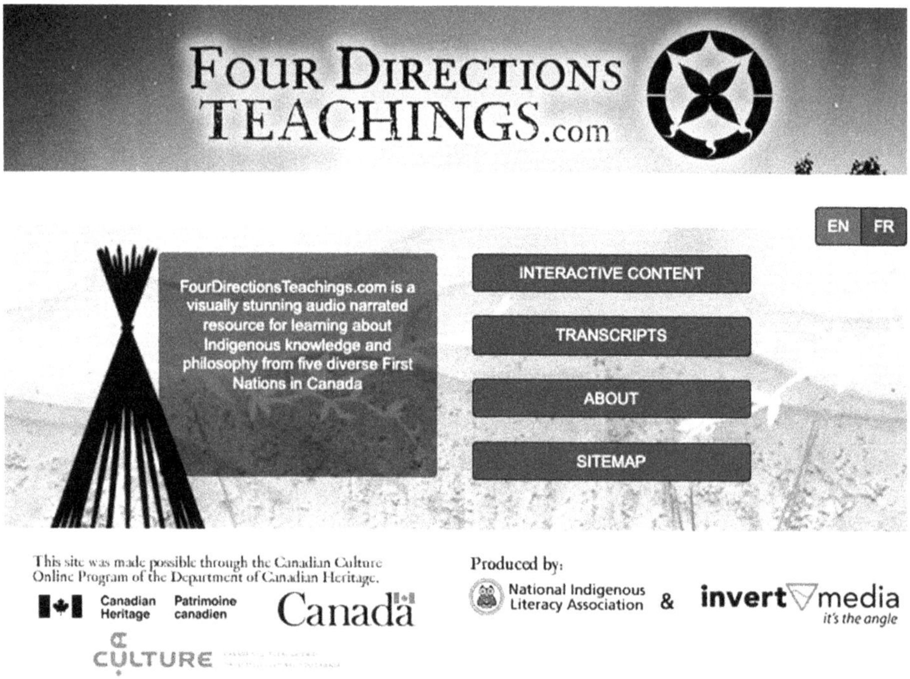

FIGURE 6.8: Screen capture of the landing page for the FourDirectionsTeachings.com website. Courtesy of the artist. © 2006–2012 All Rights Reserved 4D Interactive Inc., a subsidiary of Invert Media Inc.

to advance understanding of Indigenous worldviews via interactive multimedia content. In simple terms, FDT conveys oral teachings from Elders and Knowledge Keepers via audio narration, animation and animated visuals, diagrams, text, HTML access, as well as downloadable MP3 and PDF content. Teachings on the site include, for example, the creation of the world (Mohawk), the tipi circle model (Blackfoot), ceremony (Mi'kmaq), the medicine wheel (Cree), and the seven stages of life (Ojibwe). The experience of navigating the site is very much contingent on users' familiarity with Indigenous knowledge and on the serendipity or curiosity they harness as they navigate from one plane to the next. The immediacy achieved via these online tools is made palpable through the oral teachings (delivered by the Elders themselves) accompanied by richly animated visuals associated with each nation's respective images and imagery. As Anishinaabe educator Dr Rainey Gaywish notes of the site, 'It is the next best thing [...] to having an Elder in the classroom with you' (cited in Wemigwans 2018: 93).

There is a clear distinction to be made between a website that offers Indigenous information and one that shares Indigenous knowledge. Indeed, one of the core motivations for bringing this project into being was to counter the dearth of Indigenous knowledge websites online. Whereas Indigenous information sites are not beholden to Indigenous communities (i.e. just about anyone could create a blog or website that publishes this type of content), Indigenous knowledge sites must abide by community protocols and ethics before any material can be rightfully considered for publication. The importance of adhering to these protocols and ethics cannot be emphasized enough: based on these ideals, Wemigwans established an advisory committee that would facilitate the vetting and validation of the Indigenous knowledge to be featured on the site (2018: 167–68). The creation of advisory committees, Elder councils, and traditional councils is of the utmost importance in the act of developing Indigenous knowledge resources for the internet (2018: 101). Without them, Indigenous perspectives and teachings can be all too easily distorted and mischaracterized. Such is the case when non-Indigenous settler individuals or groups appropriate Indigenous knowledge for the purposes of commodifying and colonizing Indigenous culture, an all-too-common practice that leads to ongoing theft, misappropriation, and denigration (2018: 20–21). To safeguard against potential harm and to help ensure the project 'be undertaken in a good way' (2018: 20–21), FDT was initiated through a Sweat Lodge ceremony offered and led by the late Ojibwe Elder Lilian Pitawanakwat (whose teachings are featured on the site); this ceremonial blessing would serve to validate the proposed project and imbue the work with cultural, social, and spiritual legitimacy. The interrelated processes of establishing an advisory committee and of seeking the validation of cultural authority for the project offer two concise examples concerning the essential work to be done before Indigenous knowledge can be shared online. As Wemigwans has noted more recently, her role via FDT is to serve as a facilitator or helper in the transmission of knowledge through Knowledge Keepers and Elders (Sharma and Wemigwans 2022: 214). In offering an extensive account of her experiences building FDT, Wemigwans has shown that the act of producing Indigenous knowledge online is a multilayered, relational, community-driven, and sacred undertaking.

Far more than just a website repository for Indigenous knowledge, FDT 'is a gift of teachings that carries responsibility for the next seven generations and indeed resembles important aspects of what Traditional Teachers might call a bundle' (2018: 48). From an Indigenous perspective, a bundle refers to something sacred and/or imbued with spirit – a collection of items or things to be valued, protected, and cared for to the benefit of the community; items include smudge bowls, pipes, medicines (tobacco, dried plants), feathers, and rattles, among many others, of which many are used in specific ceremonies (2018: 34–35). A digital bundle, according to Wemigwans, refers to Indigenous knowledge bundles made available online that counter 'colonizing logics of the internet' (Sharma and Wemigwans 2022: 213), knowledge that requires care, custodianship, responsibility, and accountability on the part of its community. For Indigenous knowledge to assume such a heightened standing online is to acknowledge the potential significance of the former in advancing radical Indigenous resurgence and regeneration. Perhaps the clearest distillation of what digital bundles may offer for the future of Indigenous resurgence comes from Leanne Betasamosake Simpson (2011: 148) in *Dancing on Our Turtle's Back*, in which she speaks of Indigenous knowledge as central to the 'processes and forces of regeneration, revitalization, remembering, and visioning'. Part of what makes FDT such a powerful example is its capacity to invite Indigenous visitors of the site to (re)discover and (re)claim knowledge that was previously forbidden (Wemigwans 2018: 164) by colonial powers. Another important facet of this work connects with the larger project of decolonization in at least two viable ways. First, FDT represents a model of collaboration among Indigenous communities across Turtle Island, highlighting a core initiative to create sovereign Indigenous knowledge projects far removed from the machinations of colonial epistemologies. Second, Indigenous knowledge projects of this kind hold real potential for improving relations between Indigenous peoples and settler society. In terms of education, the site serves as an invaluable resource for both Indigenous and settler internet users. Wemigwans likens this process to 'lighting new fires' (2018: 103) for the internet and for Indigenous knowledge online as a means of education for Indigenous and settler communities. In addition to all of the teachings, FDT features a teacher's resource guide, complete with comprehensive learning activities for each bundle of teachings. These learning activities are specifically tailored to junior, intermediate, and senior students, thereby offering opportunities for both students and teachers at all levels to learn more deeply about Indigenous knowledges. For Canadian settler visitors, the website content is available in both official languages (French/English). Such website content choices are deliberate: the proliferation of Indigenous knowledge online can be leveraged for inclusion in public education systems to assist in redressing widespread ignorance surrounding Indigenous history and can also assist in mending relations between Indigenous peoples and settler society (2018: 122). In terms of resurgence, the creation of digital bundles and the expansion of Indigenous presence online may ultimately lead to the nurturing of infrastructure capable of promoting sovereign information communities produced by and for Indigenous peoples (2018: 227). Such an infrastructure would ultimately bolster access to Indigenous knowledge designed to support healing, resilience, regeneration, and futurity.

Indigenous knowledge sites such as FourDirectionsTeachings.com offer yet another lens for thinking about decolonial media imaginaries. At a time when websites have been superseded by apps and platforms as the most desirable access points for everyday online engagement, FDT proposes a welcoming virtual space for internet users to access and interface with Indigenous knowledge and philosophy in an accessible format. The site has modelled a robust framework with which Indigenous media producers can draw upon in the creation of Indigenous knowledge sites. This model is open to various kinds of collaboration, relationality, and reciprocity, and as such, it advances a distinctly Indigenous set of approaches to enacting new forms of sovereignty. Just as Wemigwans and her team facilitated the transmission of knowledge by way of Elders and Knowledge Keepers from five diverse First Nations communities, they also succeeded in bringing together different Indigenous perspectives on FDT without privileging the value of some worldviews over others. The teachings are presented as interactive content on a main navigation page that features five floating circles representing holistic approaches to Indigenous knowledge from each of the First Nations (2018: 13). The imaginaries-work at play here is significant in at least two ways. First, the image of seeing these circles suspended in space above the orb that is Turtle Island (see Figure 6.9)– Blackfoot, Cree, Ojibwe, Mohawk, and Mi'kmaq – presents an inclusive and harmonious view of how Indigenous knowledges can coexist and even offer complimentary understandings of the world. Seeing these constellations of knowledge coexist on the site creates a visually powerful expression of solidarity

FIGURE 6.9: Screen capture of the interactive content featured on the FourDirectionsTeachings.com website. Courtesy of the artist.

FIGURE 6.10: Screen capture of the multimedia content featured on the FourDirectionsTeachings.com website. Courtesy of the artist.

and sovereignty vis-à-vis each represented First Nation (see Figure 6.10). The coming together of these five nations to share Indigenous knowledge online demonstrates the underlying strength this approach may have in expanding future collaboration among other Indigenous communities not featured on the site. The second notable aspect surrounding imaginaries-work is explicitly linked to the creation of Indigenous knowledge resources and infrastructure. To be sure, nothing of its kind existed before FDT was first published, and the act of producing a website of this calibre has propelled a new way of thinking about how media producers might engage in the online transmission of Indigenous knowledge and how they might also go about creating supporting infrastructure to protect this work for generations to come. The website's existence in and of itself is emblematic of an imaginary that foresees the continued proliferation of Indigenous knowledge that addresses the needs and exigencies of various communities. The coupling together of the creation of online resources and the infrastructural supports necessary to ensure protection and longevity represents another facet of the imaginaries-work needed to inspire the next iteration of these projects.

Conclusion

This chapter's focus on the imaginaries-work of Indigenous artists has offered a window into the promise and potential of engaging Indigenous Futurisms in the articulation of decolonial politics. Through an exploration of the works of Skawennati, Jackson, and Wemigwans, I have attended to the ways in which art and media collide in manifold expressions of Indigenous resistance, sovereignty, and futurity. Video simulations, VR, and multimedia websites all offer tangible means of imagining Indigenous futures that connect to past and present understandings of the world. All three sets of examples discussed above represent the articulation of decolonial media imaginaries through the lens of Indigenous futurity, a politic that is unabashedly against seeing the future through the prism of ongoing settler-colonial power structures (Furtado 2024: 27). Importantly, there is a sense that these artists are producing works that are, in Wemigwans' words, 'deliberately designed to stand up to colonial erasure' (Wemigwans and Sharma 2022: 210) so as to ensure Indigenous resurgence. And although these media projects have almost unique applicability to ensuring the thrivance of Indigenous communities, I would also argue that the futures depicted are to be grappled with by both Indigenous and settler communities alike precisely because the proliferation of future-oriented Indigenous media imaginaries could greatly benefit both the expression and the popularization of decolonial politics.

7

Conclusion: Media Imaginaries for Reckoning, Incommensurability, and Solidarity

The ideas presented thus far have taken many detours and have enjoyed a greater degree of latitude and freedom in their expression than is usual in my writing. This project began as the formulation of a question in relation to a curiosity-inspiring concept and theoretical framework: *What future shapes, orientations, or directions might come into being with the emergence (and eventual greater proliferation) of decolonial media imaginaries?* In attempting to answer this question, I've grappled with how the latter three words – decolonial, media, imaginaries – have spawned their own histories, debates, and applications, and how such an expansive and diverse treatment of these terms has presented a number of limitations and opportunities. Indeed, *Decolonial Media Imaginaries* has engaged imaginaries-work from a decolonial perspective, seeking to present ideas both well-worn and emergent as opportunities to think more deeply on the promise and potential of images and imaginaries in contributing to the larger project of decolonial politics. The question of where exactly *media* fit within this three-word formulation remains open for consideration. Originally inspired by Sundar and Mukherjee's (2022: 1) provocation to conceive of decolonial feminisms as an invitation to 'enter midstream, in medias res' – I have accepted the call to reorient myself away from conventional ways of positioning myself vis-à-vis our areas of study, fields, and disciplines to focus more acutely on the mechanisms and levers needed to better articulate the decolonial politics to come. Entering midstream is one surefire (albeit oblique) way of contributing to an ever-growing body of decolonial scholarship and thought dedicated to freedom struggles and emancipation projects the world over.

My approach has been to raise questions about the suitability, viability, and manoeuvrability of media imaginaries as potential modes of intervention capable of advancing ways of feeling, thinking, discussing, and relating to the prospect of living decolonial futures. In more formal terms, I've incorporated ideas surrounding spectacle and display (World's Fair), corporatized technological fantasy (televisual advertising), energy infrastructure (solarities), community-centred storytelling (salmon project), social media movements (#RhodesMustFall), pedagogical reparations (film and media studies curricula), artworld decolonial praxis (Chapter 5), and Indigenous media futures (Chapter 6). In bringing together these seemingly disparate examples, I've attempted to show how the decolonial project of the present and future is connected to virtually all realms of existence, and that the imaginaries-work that is currently animating and informing this project can be found in a variety of different communities, spaces, and contexts. Although countless other companion examples could be integrated here, this small constellation of ideas has inspired me to draw some preliminary conclusions regarding the potential uses and contributions of decolonial media imaginaries-work: namely, that the latter is capable of prompting reflection, inciting dialogue, instigating action, and deepening relationality. Future studies could explore (and validate) the legitimacy of this claim, but what I really want to address in these final pages is the extent to which decolonial media imaginaries exist as levers and/or mechanisms for signalling the immediacy of engaging with interlocking notions of reckoning, incommensurability, and solidarity as foundational to the present and future of decolonial political struggle.

Reckoning

To say that we are witnessing the end of times and/or the coming of the apocalypse is to brazenly dismiss the reality that the Indigenous peoples of Turtle Island have long inhabited the apocalyptic and dystopian futures that are imminently upon us – those exacerbated by the expansion of colonialism and settler capitalism to the far reaches of the planet (Whyte 2017). Scores of scholars have tied the ecological collapse and environmental demise of the current moment to the continued hegemony of modernity, capitalism, and heteropatriarchy. Together, all three systems of dominance have worked to ensure the foreclosure of any competing systems or ways of living and being, just as they have operated in the interests of enforcing the broader view that human progress is an undeniable and inalienable force guiding all of our collective activities. To put it crudely, in accepting these systems of dominance as overarching forces in the articulation of life on this planet, we have agreed to the terms in fine print that clearly state there will be winners and losers, of which the winners will comprise a select few, with the losers comprising the vast majority. Among the losers are the earth's living species, both human and more-than-human. One of the most powerful responses to this current state of affairs has been articulated through calls for a profound reckoning with the neocolonial societies of the present. The first of these calls to rattle the popular imagination would emerge in April 2020, in a widely read essay by author and activist Arundhati Roy. In 'The pandemic is a portal', Roy painstakingly describes the injustices, inequities, and inequalities exacerbated by the COVID-19 pandemic in India, a context in which society's most vulnerable are left to navigate the fallout without meaningful assistance of any kind (2020). If anything, Roy lays bare the even harsher reality that many of the most vulnerable people she spoke to at the outset of the pandemic had already been facing looming unemployment, starvation, and police violence. Unwilling to accept the suffering of others as an inevitable externality, and dismissive of the idea of a future return to normality, Roy argues that the pandemic is 'a portal, a gateway between one world and the next', a portal 'we can walk through lightly, with little luggage, ready to imagine another world. And ready to fight for it' (2020: n.pag.).

A second powerful call to reckon would appear a few months later in July 2020, in an essay written by poet, novelist, and scholar, Dionne Brand. In 'On narrative, reckoning and the calculus of living and dying', Brand urges her readers to be weary of the rhetoric associated with 'when things return to normal' – a phrase often used during the pandemic to invoke a time in the not-so-distant future in which the normalcy and comfort of the pre-pandemic would be restored for all. To which Brand categorically rejects the normalcy embedded in the era's benign ordering of contemporary life:

> Was the violence against women normal? Was the anti-Black and anti-Indigenous racism normal? Was white supremacy normal? Was the homelessness growing on the streets normal? Were homophobia and transphobia normal? Were pervasive surveillance and policing of Black and Indigenous and people of colour normal?
> (2020: n. pag.)

In the face of these ongoing forms of oppression, as experienced through the slowed-down temporalities reinforced through interlocking shutdowns, Brand would lob a beautiful provocation: 'The reckoning might be now'. Both Brand and Roy's respective accounts of life lived under deeply oppressive conditions during the early stages of the pandemic instigated a broader call for a widespread reckoning capable of reimagining the world along radically new lines.

Of particular interest here is the way that calls for reckoning are interwoven with the cultivation of images and in the elaboration of imaginaries. In an interview that appeared shortly after the publication of Brand's essay, Saidiya Hartman invoked an abolitionist imaginary as a portal towards more just futures; such an invocation 'requires the abolition of the carceral world, the abolition of capitalism.

What is required is a remaking of the social order, and nothing short of that is going to make a difference' (Damman 2020). To reckon, according to Hartman, is to simultaneously abolish oppressive forces, structures, and institutions, and engage in a 'wild exercise of imagination' as precursor to bringing bold new worlds into being. Maynard and Simpson have also clearly delineated the relationship between abolition and imagination, arguing that abolition and anticolonial struggle are deeply embedded in the realm of 'imagination work, conjure work, science fiction in real time' (2022: 176). Inspired by Roy's allusion to the pandemic portal, they also describe the attendant risks associated with reckoning and abolition work; indeed, the risks of remaking the social order and of committing full-stop to the decolonization of life on this planet will signal the end of safety (Maynard and Simpson 2022: 253). Traversing the portal will represent elements of risk, but for peoples whose futures have long been foreclosed by dominant interests, the risks seem minimal when compared to what they have already endured. Calls to reckon are also being made in the service of refusing dispossession, rejecting settler colonialism, and putting an end to the violence of capitalism, white supremacy, heteropatriarchy, and anti-Blackness; as Simpson argues, one strategy for bringing these changes to light involves 'resurgent humans and nonhumans radically imagining their ways out of domination, who are not afraid to let those imaginings destroy the pillars of settler colonialism' (2017: 10). For Vanessa Machado de Oliveira (2021: 18), the reckoning to be done must involve facing up to the dark side of modernity and coloniality (interlocking matrices), which continues to engender dispossession, expropriation, extraction, militarization, ecocides, and genocides. Reckoning involves divesting and disinvesting from modernity/coloniality, and one vital element needed to carry out this work is storytelling. Stories as tools for reckoning, she writes, 'might help us put expired stories to rest [e.g. modernity/colonialism]; and to sense, relate, and imagine otherwise' (2021: 16). In *Against Purity*, Alexis Shotwell (2016: 10) engages the question of reckoning through a broader recognition of 'the impossibility of purity' in an era marked by our complicity in ongoing historical injustices (e.g. settler colonialism); for Shotwell, we must not only 'reckon with realizing our entanglement and vulnerability in the world' (2016: 154), we must collectively develop new prefigurative narratives powerful enough to enact new norms and ways of living and being. The elaboration of new norms via narrative (what Shotwell calls 'open normativities') can help prepare the way for multispecies (human and more-than-human) flourishing. Shotwell is also careful to underline that reckoning must account for the unjust past, the interdependent present, and the unforeseeable future before any meaningful practice of collective liberation can transpire. These forms of reckoning, recognition, and accountability through imagination, stories, and narrative hold a great deal of potential in forging new paths towards decolonial futures.

Incommensurability

Despite the growing proliferation of calls for reckoning and accountability, we must also grapple with the divergent politics embedded across the much broader terrain of decolonial struggle. As I mentioned in the book's introduction, the work of decolonization is impossible without first acknowledging an ethic of incommensurability. Returning once again to Tuck and Yang, they argue that 'decolonization is accountable to Indigenous sovereignty and futurity' and as such, settlers must relinquish their stranglehold on the dominant imaginary of perpetual futurity, all the while relieving themselves of the false promise that 'settlers may one day be commensurable to Native peoples' (2012: 36). In a previous discussion of 'Canada 150' in Chapter 5, I noted that the theme of reconciliation was selected for the year-long event without consultation with Indigenous groups, in what amounts to a soft and insidious example of how the nation state's interests are always advanced to push forward its own political agenda, often to the detriment of Indigenous communities. Even in instances when an ethic of commensurability is implied – here through the invocation of the term reconciliation – the nation state's priorities are nowhere aligned with Indigenous objectives of achieving sovereignty and self-determination. One might argue that the friction produced on the part of the nation state is at once clear and deliberate precisely because the latter wishes to infer a sense of good will in their relations with First Nations and Indigenous communities without having to live up to their statements and commitments. For example, in 2008 former Prime Minister Steven Harper issued a long-awaited formal apology for Canada's role in the Indian Residential School system only to deny a year later that Canada has any history of colonialism (Shotwell 2016: 31). In 2016, the Trudeau Government announced that it would be acting on 41 of the 45 federal recommendations enshrined in the Truth and Reconciliation Report (Beaumont 2017), but one of the defining signatures of his government has been to voice his support for reconciliation efforts in the same breath as he has used 'government force to override Aboriginal will' (Lim 2020: n.pag.). Nowhere has this dissonance been more evident than through his support for the Coastal GasLink pipeline and the expansion of the tar sands pipeline (Trans Mountain), despite enormous public protest and unrelenting resistance by Indigenous communities across the country. Consultation with Indigenous groups for these and other extractivist projects offer a distillation of how colonial power is expressed via the nation state. As Subhabrata Bobby Banerjee (2022) explains, the very seat of contradiction between Indigenous sovereignty and ongoing colonialism lies in the disavowal of land rights in places like Australia, Canada, and other settler colonies. He asks: 'what does "meaningful consultation" mean when resource extraction projects can still proceed without "agreement of tribal leaders?"' (Banerjee 2022:

291). The blatant hypocrisy here is that nation states are all too seasoned in making commitments to reconciliation and to presenting an agenda to decolonize settler colonial society at the same time that they are contributing to the dispossession and erasure of Indigenous peoples. Needless to say, the Canadian nation state's commitment to reconciliation is extremely fraught, and recent history suggests that incommensurability is the most apt term to describe relations between the settler state and Indigenous communities.

Despite the creation of alliances between Indigenous peoples and other minority and ethnic groups, justice is sought on fundamentally different fronts: whereas the latter seek inclusion and equality in their struggles for greater recognition, Indigenous communities continue to fight to achieve sovereignty and independence from the colonial nation state (Arvin et al. 2013: 10). As Arvin et al. (2013) have argued, these concerns come to the fore in feminist alliance-building collaborations when Indigenous women, women of colour, and white women experience conflict when themes of equ(al)ity and parity do not align with issues surrounding sovereignty. Incommensurability remains a defining element when we confront the complexity of decolonial politics and the articulation of Indigenous futures. It is not simply a question of acknowledging that Indigenous futurity is incommensurable with settler colonialism and settler capitalism, it is also a matter of admitting our ongoing complicity in these systemic structures. According to Machado de Oliveira,

> decolonization is impossible when our livelihoods are underwritten by colonial violence and unsustainability. The food we eat, the clothes we wear, our health systems and social security, and the technologies that allow us to read and write about this are all subsidized by expropriation, dispossession, destitution, genocides, and ecocides. There is no way around it.
>
> (2021: 244)

Despite the apparent irreconcilable nature of these social and political arrangements, optimism persists surrounding the present and future collaborations between Indigenous and non-Indigenous peoples. Roopika Risam (2022) has shown that although extractive practices within the realm of education, media, and activism continue to shape how settlers benefit from their complicity in upholding settler colonialism, decolonial feminist activist praxis (e.g. #MMIW) has modelled how 'redistributive currency' connects the vital work of Indigenous activists on both the local and international stage. Eve Tuck and Rubén Gaztambide-Fernández insist that commitments to Indigenous futurity do not foreclose the presence or participation of non-Indigenous peoples, they only 'foreclose settler colonialism and settler epistemologies' (2013: 80). Advancing this position one step further,

T. J. Demos (2023b: 16) argues that incommensurability does not leave settlers and Indigenous peoples at odds, but rather recognizes uncommonality and difference in shared struggle. Framed in a slightly different register, this could also materialize by way of expressing an interest in common that is not the same interest (Blaser and de la Cadena 2018: 12). For Demos, the question then becomes: 'How do we become political accomplices [across difference]?' ('Decolonize This Place'). The key to answering this question may rest on the viability and cultivation of solidarity.

Solidarity (and multispecies freedom)

Having discussed the call for reckoning and in situating the challenges associated with incommensurability, I now turn to solidarity as a necessary means for engaging in the proliferation of emancipatory imaginaries and in the deepening of decolonial ties and relations. In an oft-cited passage, Sara Ahmed offers an insightful segue between the conceptual intricacies of moving between solidarity and incommensurability:

> Solidarity does not assume that our struggles are the same struggles, or that our pain is the same pain, or that our hope is for the same future. Solidarity involves commitment, and work, as well as the recognition that even if we do not have the same feelings, or the same lives, or the same bodies, we do live on common ground.
> (2014: 189)

Our struggles may differ and diverge but we do live in relation (on common ground) and our efforts to bring about better worlds may be interwoven. For settlers, this requires some acknowledgement that even the most well-intentioned efforts can still work to deflect responsibility, conceal guilt, and shore up power, especially when land, privilege, and power are concerned (Tuck and Yang 2012: 21). For everyone else, Imani Perry's exploration of personhood under patriarchy invites an essential question: 'How can we be something other than neoliberal subjects?' (2018: 229) – and how can new maps and imaginaries contribute to the hope and future of liberation, more broadly? The prospects of living in solidarity beyond the all-consuming constraints and pressures associated with neo-liberalism and colonialism offer a veritable mixed bag of potential outcomes. For Su-ming Khoo and Anique Vered (2020: 233, 225), the goal is twofold: first, to acknowledge that spaces of decoloniality can involve difficult processes, painful interactions, and uneasy relations; and second, to engage in this solidarity-work as an opportunity to move beyond colonial haunting in seeking 'other ways of being bound-together'. In *Otherwise Worlds: Against Settler Colonialism and Anti-Blackness*, King et al. (2020) address the very real complexities at the heart of relations between Black and Indigenous peoples in the express interests of theorizing a relationality beyond incommensurability and antagonism towards something more akin to solidarity. As they see it, 'Black and Native communities must talk about and come to terms with the reality that Black and Native collectives who negotiate their terms of survival with settler states are forced to compromise the well-being of the other' (2020: 8), a state of affairs that makes solidarity difficult, if not impossible. They argue that one strategy to bolster solidarity and to deepen relationality is to resist the act of seeking 'redress and healing through the settler state' and instead to ruminate together on 'what healing and redress would look like on otherwise or decolonial and abolitionist terms' (King et al. 2020: 8; see Coulthard 2014). Contributing to this line of inquiry, Maynard and Simpson (2022: 94) identify the tensions underpinning Black and Indigenous justice projects and frame them through both abolitionist and settler colonial lenses to establish greater visibility of/for political affinities between both communities. In confronting shared histories of the centuries-long impacts of white supremacy, settler violence, and genocide, the pain and indignities of both current and previous epochs will undoubtedly make collaboration an uneasy undertaking. However, these uneasy attempts to sew together a shared relationality built upon visions of interdependent forms of freedom may give way to what Haraway has called 'frictionful solidarity' (cited in Demos 2023b: 156). Despite the perceived challenges associated with forging incommensurable paths (and possibly incompatible political projects), goals of shared liberation bring other elements to light. Murri artist Lilla Watson's famous passage concerning solidarity-work is noteworthy in this regard: 'If you have come to help me, then you are wasting your time. But if you have come because your liberation is bound up with mine, then let us work together' (cited in Shotwell 2016: 203). The promise of interlocking vistas of liberation seems like the very glue needed to make solidarity ties stick as far and as widely as possible. Building even more broadly on this idea, Hazel Carby poses the following question as it relates to the unfinished projects of liberation and freedom: 'Could we become capacious enough to build solidarity not only across binaries of gender and borders of race, ethnicities, indigeneity and nation to include all species?' (2020: n.pag.). According to many, solidarity as expressed through the interdependence of all species is what's needed to bring about the decolonial futures of tomorrow (Kimmerer 2013; Puig de la Bellacasa 2017; Shotwell 2016). In the words of Ruha Benjamin, 'Solidarity takes interdependence seriously' (2019: 194). On one level, solidarity struggles working to abolish settler colonialism and anti-Blackness are vital to ensuring survivance, joy, and relationality (King et al. 2020: 10). On another level, they are also key to bringing about different kinds of resurgence and interdependent flourishing. As Catherine E. Walsh illustrates, interdependent solidarity is akin to

> seeds taking root and flowers beginning to bloom within a whole series of cracks and fissures that extend across cement and stone walls and earthen territories, weaving in and out, making and showing their relationality and connections, resisting and (re)existing, and continuing the work to decolonize and deschool.
>
> (2023: 118)

Seeds, roots, and flowers have as much to teach us about relationality as they do about creating and expanding cracks and fissures in undesirable colonial (infra) structures. Whether you take Walsh on either metaphoric or literal terms, her depiction of decolonial paths both above and below the surface offer an important relay between the crack-making solidarity-work to be done and the elements of interdependent flourishing that will follow. For Mvskoke scholar Laura Harjo, engaging in deeper commitments to solidarity-work may lay the groundwork for multispecies flourishing that leads to an emancipation away from settler imaginaries, ideologies, and practices and towards decolonial futurities that generate 'a trajectory that has a beautiful path to a lush place' (cited in King et al. 2020: 13). A decolonial imaginaries blueprint and/or recipe: seeds, roots, flowers, beautiful paths, and lush places.

Moving from states of reckoning to acknowledgements of incommensurability to expressions of deeper forms of solidarity is no small undertaking. We may not know how to cultivate lasting solidarity with one another or to express solidarity across difference, but we will need to work tirelessly to figure this out if we wish to survive collectively. As Demos insists, a precondition for maintaining and enhancing solidarity will be to shore up fidelity across identities, differences, borders, and species, and to develop a framework of 'universality premised on the unconditional emancipation of all' (2023b: 216–18). The work to build decolonial futures will rest on the creation of collective care networks; by the same token, the proliferation of these networks will depend on the creation of new caring imaginaries, which may only be activated once we come to terms with our shared entanglement, vulnerability, and interdependence (Chatzidakis et al. 2020; Butler 2020). Even more profoundly, we will need to develop relations based on radical tenderness and in a political practice of healing, a shift that involves unlearning our ways 'of thinking and imagining; of sensing and feeling; of relating to one another, the earth, and the cosmos; of facing life, fear, pain, loss, and death' (Machado de Oliveira 2021: xxi). On the question of what is to be done both now and in the future, Machado de Oliveira is the most convincing and insightful. In addition to engaging in a full-on reckoning with, and severance from, modernity, she argues that we must contribute to a clearing and decluttering of our arrogant ways, entitlements, and securities; we must also prioritize periods of gestation and the cultivation of the 'creative imagination' (Machado de Oliveira 2021: 240) as a necessary means for producing and proliferating 'decolonial gestures' (2021: 244).

Of the diverse examples alluded to in these pages – including, but not limited to, the running of the salmon project, solar infrastructure, media futures, institutional critique and reform – I would readily refer to the latter as decolonial gestures operating in the service of decolonial imaginaries. In writing *Decolonial Media Imaginaries*, I have attempted to decentre enduring imaginaries rooted in colonial, capitalist, and neo-liberal fantasies about what constitutes the good life, in favour of centring decolonial imaginaries that redraw the lines of possibility surrounding emancipatory futures for human and more-than-human worlds. Adapting Mosco's (2004) notion of myths as being either living or dead, there is a sense that decolonial imaginaries must, first and foremost, become living, animated, and animating fixtures in contemporary life, and second, must contribute, bit by bit, to the transformation of our ways of living and being. At their most powerful, decolonial media imaginaries could offer new desire lines and lines of flight for us to follow. In a beautiful passage that describes the power and transcendence of Anishinaabe artist Rebecca Belmore, Simpson writes: 'She is both the presence and the doorway, and in her performances she often gives birth to the flight paths out of settler colonial reality and then literally takes those flight paths in front of the audience as witness' (2017: 203). Following Belmore's example, the actors, collectives, communities, movements, and institutions discussed in this book share not only the capacity to deploy imaginaries-work in the creation of paths beyond settler colonialism, they also share the possibility of illuminating for others how to create decolonial futures of their own. Following Gloria Anzaldúa (2015: 44–45), the creation of new imaginaries for ourselves and others assists in healing 'colonialism's wounds', while also participating in the building of new realities and otherwise worlds. Although interventions of this kind represent but a small piece of the work to be done on the paths to decolonization, they constitute vital, dynamic, and transformative contributions to this broader project.

On a final note, a future without media or imaginaries is impossible to grasp, and as such, their respective roles cannot be understated in the re-visioning of our current context. If our decolonial media imaginaries have the capacity to channel all the light and promise of our contemporary imaginaries – minus the all-depleting and cataclysmic properties they currently espouse – we may begin to invigorate processes of renewal, resurgence, and interdependence among relations for a world marked by multispecies flourishing.

Bibliography

9 Weeks of Art in Action (n.d.), 'Decolonize this place', https://decolonizethisplace.org/9weeksofartinaction2. Accessed 17 March 2025.

After Oil Collective (2022), *Solarities: Seeking Energy Justice*, Minneapolis: University of Minnesota Press.

Ahmed, A. Kayum (2020), '#RhodesMustFall: How a decolonial student movement in the Global South inspired epistemic disobedience at the University of Oxford', *African Studies Review*, 63:2, pp. 281–303, https://doi.org/10.1017/asr.2019.49.

Ahmed, Sara (2006), *Queer Phenomenology: Orientations, Objects, Others*, Durham, NC: Duke University Press.

Ahmed, Sara (2014), *The Cultural Politics of Emotion*, 2nd ed., Edinburgh: Edinburgh University Press.

Ahmed, Sara (2017), *Living a Feminist Life,* Durham, NC: Duke University Press.

Ahmed, Sara (2019), *What's the Use?: On the Uses of Use,* Durham, NC: Duke University Press.

Ahmed, Sara (2021), *Complaint!,* Durham, NC: Duke University Press.

Allaire, Christian (2020), 'This indigenous artist designs traditional clothes for a virtual world', *Vogue*, 26 August, https://www.vogue.com/article/skawennati-indigenous-artist-virtual-fashion. Accessed 17 March 2025.

Alteveer, Ian, Beachler, Hannah, Lawrence, Sarah and Commander, Michelle D. (2022), *Before Yesterday We Could Fly: An Afrofuturist Period Room*, New York: Metropolitan Museum of Art.

Anon. (2019), 'Climate leaders don't build pipelines', *CBC News*, 22 May, https://www.cbc.ca/news/canada/british-columbia/trudeau-vancouver-indigenous-leader-confrontation-1.5145671. Accessed 17 March 2025.

Anon. (2022), 'Mark the 150th anniversary of Confederation with a funding program for commemoration projects on theme of reconciliation', *CBC News*, 17 June, https://www.cbc.ca/newsinteractives/beyond-94/mark-the-150th-anniversary-of-confederation-with-a-funding-program-for-commemoration-projects-on-theme -of-reconciliation. Accessed 17 March 2025.

Anzaldúa, Gloria (2015), *Light in the Dark = Luz en lo oscuro: Rewriting Identity, Spirituality, Reality* (ed. A. Keating), Durham, NC: Duke University Press.

Ariese, Csilla and Wróblewska, Magdalena (2021), *Practicing Decoloniality in Museums: A Guide with Global Examples*, Amsterdam: Amsterdam University Press.

Arvin, Maile (2015), 'Analytics of indigeneity', in S. N. Teves, A. Smith and M. H. Raheja (eds), *Native Studies Keywords*, Tucson: University of Arizona Press, pp. 119–29.

Arvin, Maile, Tuck, Eve and Morrill, Angie (2013), 'Decolonizing feminism: Challenging connections between settler colonialism and heteropatriarchy', *Feminist Formations*, 25:1, pp. 8–34, https://doi.org/10.1353/ff.2013.0006.

Assis, Mariana Prandini, Forrest, Michelle, Henderson, Angela, MacCallum, Lindsey, Reilly, Ian, Shaffner, Ellen and Stoneman, Scott (2023), *Widening Scripts: Cultivating Feminist Care in Academic Labor*, Brooklyn: punctum books.

AT&T (1993), 'You Will' Ads, YouTube, https://www.youtube.com/watch?v=TZb0avfQme8. Accessed 17 March 2025.

Auerbach, Jeffrey (1999), *The Great Exhibition of 1851: A Nation on Display*, New Haven: Yale University Press.

Balkissoon, Denise (2018), 'A virtual-reality film that imagines Toronto's wild future', *The Globe and Mail*, 21 December, https://www.theglobeandmail.com/canada/toronto/article-a-virtual-reality-film-that-imagines-torontos-wild-future/. Accessed 17 March 2025.

Banerjee, Subhabrata Bobby (2022), 'Decolonizing deliberative democracy: Perspectives from below', *Journal of Business Ethics*, 181:2, pp. 283–99, https://doi.org/10.1007/s10551-021-04971-5.

Barnard, Elissa (2023), 'Affecting the past and changing the present: Tyshan Wright's Maroon Town', *Billie*, 8 December, https://billiemag.ca/affecting-the-past-and-changing-the-present-tyshan-wrights-maroon-town/. Accessed 17 March 2025.

Barney, Darin (2017), 'Who we are and what we do: Canada as a pipeline nation', in S. Wilson, A. Carlson and I. Szeman (eds), *Petrocultures: Oil, Politics, Culture*, Montreal: McGill-Queen's University Press, pp. 78–119, https://doi.org/10.1515/9780773550391-006.

Barthes, Roland (1957), *Mythologies*, Paris: Éditions du Seuil.

Basseches, Josh (2022), 'Afterword', in *Kent Monkman: Being Legendary*, Toronto: Art Canada Institute, pp. 162–164.

Beaule, Christine D. (2017), *Frontiers of Colonialism*, Gainesville: University Press of Florida.

Beaumont, Hilary (2017), 'Fact check: How much progress has Trudeau actually made on promises to Indigenous people?' *VICE*, 25 January, https://www.vice.com/en/article/fact-check-how-much-progress-has-trudeau-actually-made-on-promises-to-indigenous-people/. Accessed 17 March 2025.

Bellrichard, Chantelle and Barrera, Jorge (2020), 'What you need to know about the Coastal GasLink pipeline conflict', *CBC News*, 5 February, https://www.cbc.ca/news/indigenous/wet-suwet-en-coastal-gaslink-pipeline-1.5448363. Accessed 17 March 2025.

Benjamin, Ruha (2019), *Race After Technology: Abolitionist Tools for the New Jim Code*, Cambridge: Polity.

Bennett, Tony (1988), 'The exhibitionary complex', *New Formations*, 4, pp. 73–102, https://journals.lwbooks.co.uk/newformations/vol-1988-issue-4/abstract-7713/. Accessed 17 March 2025.

Bennett, Tony (1991), 'The shaping of things to come: Expo '88', *Cultural Studies*, 5:1, pp. 30–51, https://doi.org/10.1080/09502389100490031.

Berg, Maggie and Seeber, Barbara K. (2016), *The Slow Professor: Challenging the Culture of Speed in the Academy*, Toronto: University of Toronto Press.

Bernal, Victoria (2021), 'Digitality and decolonization: A response to Achille Mbembe', *African Studies Review*, 64:1, pp. 41–56, https://doi.org/10.1017/asr.2020.90.

Blaser, Mario and de la Cadena, Marisol (eds) (2020), 'Pluriverse: Proposals for a world of many worlds', in *A World of Many Worlds*, Durham, NC: Duke University Press, pp. 1–22, https://doi.org/10.1515/9781478004318-002.

Bolin, Göran (2019), 'Generational "we-sense", "they-sense" and narrative: An epistemological approach to media and social change', *EMPIRIA: Revista de Metodología de Ciencias Sociales*, 0:42, pp. 21–36, https://doi.org/10.5944/empiria.42.2019.23249.

Bon, Anna, Dittoh, Francis, Lô, Gossa, Pini, Monica, Bwana, Robert, WaiShiang, Cheah, Kulathuramaiyer, Narayanan and Baart, Andre (2022), 'Decolonizing technology and society: A perspective from the Global South', in H. Werthner, E. Prem, E. A. Lee and C. Ghezzi (eds), *Perspectives on Digital Humanism*, Cham: Springer International Publishing, pp. 61–68.

Bouraly, Lisa (2019), 'L'histoire du Canada revue et corrigée par l'artiste autochtone Kent Monkman', *The Conversation*, 8 February, http://theconversation.com/lhistoire-du-canada-revue-et-corrigee-par-lartiste-autochtone-kent-monkman-110968. Accessed 17 March 2025.

Brah, Avtar (2022), *Decolonial Imaginings: Intersectional Conversations and Contestations*, London: Goldsmiths Press.

Brand, Dionne (2020), 'On narrative, reckoning and the calculus of living and dying', *Toronto Star*, 4 July, https://www.thestar.com/entertainment/books/dionne-brand-on-narrative-reckoning-and-the-calculus-of-living-and-dying/article_47884274-07ad-561a-973b-027ef2cbc8fb.html. Accessed 17 March 2025.

Brennan, Shane (2017), 'Visionary infrastructure: Community solar streetlights in Highland Park', *Journal of Visual Culture*, 16:2, pp. 167–89, https://doi.org/10.1177/1470412916685743.

Brown, Kate (2022a), 'Risks come with the concept': Documenta 15's curators reflect on a controversial, history-making show', *Artnet News*, 21 September, https://news.artnet.com/art-world/documenta-15-ruangrupa-2179250. Accessed 17 March 2025.

Brown, Kate (2022b), '"We take ownership and responsibility": Indonesian collective Taring Padi reflects on the controversy over their art that paralyzed Documenta', *Artnet News*, 9 August, https://news.artnet.com/art-world-archives/taring-padi-collective-interview-2155080. Accessed 17 March 2025.

Butler, Judith (2020), *The Force of Nonviolence: An Ethico-Political Bind*, London: Verso Books.

Carby, Hazel (2020), 'Black futurities: Shape-shifting beyond the limits of the human', *InVisible Culture*, 31, https://doi.org/10.47761/494a02f6.cb3aaba1.

Carlson, Bronwyn (2023), 'The future is indigenous', in M. Day, S. O'Sullivan and T. Kennedy (eds), *The Routledge Handbook of Australian Indigenous Peoples and Futures*, London: Routledge, pp. 9–25, https://doi.org/10.4324/9781003271802.

Carney, Sean J. Patrick (2017), 'Taking up space: An interview with the Wood Land School', *ARTnews*, 30 October, https://www.artnews.com/art-in-america/interviews/taking-up-space-an-interview-with-the-wood-land-school-56444/. Accessed 17 March 2025.

Causevic, Az, Philip, Kavita, Zwick-Maitreyi, Maari, Lewis, Persephone Hooper, Bouterse, Siko and Sengupta, Anasuya (2020), 'Centering knowledge from the margins: Our embodied practices of epistemic resistance and revolution', *International Feminist Journal of Politics*, 22:1, pp. 6–25, https://doi.org/10.1080/14616742.2019.1701515.

Cecco, Leyland (2024), 'Canada hands "long-overdue" title over more than 200 islands to Haida Nation', *The Guardian*, 15 April, https://www.theguardian.com/world/2024/apr/15/haida-first-nation-land-canada. Accessed 17 March 2025.

Chakravartty, Paula, Kuo, Rachel, Grubbs, Victoria and McIlwain, Charlton (2018), '#CommunicationSoWhite', *Journal of Communication*, 68:2, pp. 254–66, https://doi.org/10.1093/joc/jqy003.

Charland, Maurice (1986), 'Technological nationalism', *Canadian Journal of Political and Social Theory*, 10:1&2, pp. 196–220.

Chatzidakis, Andreas, Hakim, Jamie, Littler, Jo, Rottenberg, Catherine and Segal, Lynne (2020), *The Care Manifesto: The Politics of Interdependence*, London: Verso Books.

Chiumbu, Sarah H. and Radebe, Mandla (2020), 'Towards a Decolonial Critical Political Economy of the Media: Some Initial Thoughts', *Communicatio: South African Journal for Communication Theory and Research*, 6:1, pp. 1–20, doi:10.1080/02500167.2020.1757931.

Collins, Leah (2022), 'His ancestors were forbidden from bringing their instruments to Canada; that's why he makes them today', *CBC Arts*, 22 July, https://www.cbc.ca/arts/sobey-art-award-q-a-tyshan-wright-1.6527843. Accessed 17 March 2025.

Comaroff, Jean and Comaroff, John (2012), *Theory from the South: Or, How Euro-America is Evolving Toward Africa*, London: Routledge, https://doi.org/10.4324/9781315631639.

Cooppan, Vilashini (2019), 'Time-maps: A field guide to the decolonial imaginary', *Critical Times*, 2:3, pp. 396–415, https://doi.org/10.1215/26410478-7862533.

Couldry, Nick and Mejias, Ulises A. (2019), *The Costs of Connection: How Data Is Colonizing Human Life and Appropriating It for Capitalism*, Stanford: Stanford University Press, https://doi.org/10.1515/9781503609754.

Coulthard, Glen Sean (2014), *Red Skin, White Masks: Rejecting the Colonial Politics of Recognition*, Minneapolis: University of Minnesota Press.

Crawford, Kate (2021), *Atlas of AI: Power, Politics, and the Planetary Costs of Artificial Intelligence*, New Haven: Yale University Press.

Crawford, Kate and Joler, Vladan (2019), 'Anatomy of an AI system', *Virtual Creativity*, 9:1, pp. 117–20, https://doi.org/10.1386/vcr_00008_7.

Crawford, Tiffany (2018), 'Trudeau calls LNG project in B.C. the biggest private investment in Canada's history', *Vancouver Sun*, 2 October, https://vancouversun.com/news/local-news/trudeau-calls-lng-project-in-b-c-biggest-private-investment-in-canadas-history. Accessed 17 March 2025.

Crawford-Holland, Sasha and LeBlanc, Lindsay (2023), 'Making things our [digital] own": Lessons on time and sovereignty from Indigenous computational art', in D. Claxton and E. Winton (eds), *Indigenous Media Arts in Canada: Making, Caring, Sharing*, Waterloo: Wilfrid Laurier University Press, pp. 324–49, https://doi.org/10.51644/9781771125437-016.

Damman, Catherine (2020), 'Interviews: Saidiya Hartman', *Artforum*, 14 July, https://www.artforum.com/columns/saidiya-hartman-on-insurgent-histories-and-the-abolitionist-imaginary-248115. Accessed 17 March 2025.

Dawson, Ashley (2022), *Extinction: A Radical History*, New York: OR Books.

Day, Pip (2017), 'When the colonizer comes to stay', in O. Paul, S. Lucy and W. Mick (eds), *How Institutions Think: Between Contemporary Art and Curatorial Discourse*, Cambridge, MA: MIT Press, pp. 85–99.

de Bruyn, Eric C. H. (2023), 'Missed encounters: Introduction to Documenta 15 Dossier', *Grey Room*, 92, pp. 64–73, https://doi.org/10.1162/grey_a_00379. Accessed 17 March 2025.

Dechausay, Lucius (2018), 'Imagine if Toronto were reclaimed by nature. This Indigenous futurism VR experience takes you there', *CBC Arts*, 18 September, https://www.cbc.ca/arts/exhibitionists/imagine-if-toronto-were-reclaimed-by-nature-this-indigenous-futurism-vr-experience-takes-you-there-1.4828320. Accessed 17 March 2025.

Decter, Leah and Taunton, Carla (2022), 'Embodying decolonial methodology: Building and sustaining critical relationality in the cultural sector', in E. Morton (ed.), *Unsettling Canadian Art History*, Montreal: McGill-Queen's University Press, pp. 87–111.

Demos, T. J. (2023a), 'On Documenta 15', *Grey Room*, 92, pp. 125–30, https://doi.org/10.1162/grey_a_00378.

Demos, T. J. (2023b), *Radical Futurisms: Ecologies of Collapse, Chronopolitics and Justice-to-Come*, Berlin: Sternberg Press.

Dillon, Grace L. (ed.) (2012), *Walking the Clouds: An Anthology of Indigenous Science Fiction*, Tuscon: University of Arizona Press.

Dillon, Grace L. (2016), 'Indigenous futurisms, Bimaashi Biidaas mose, flying and walking towards you', *Extrapolation*, 57:1&2, pp. 1–6, https://doi.org/10.3828/extr.2016.2.

Doctorow, Cory (2023), 'The "Enshittification" of TikTok', *Wired*, 23 January, https://www.wired.com/story/tiktok-platforms-cory-doctorow/. Accessed 17 March 2025.

Dowling, Emma (2021), *The Care Crisis: What Caused It and How Can We End It?*, London: Verso Books.

Duarte, Marisa Elena (2017), *Network Sovereignty: Building the Internet Across Indian Country*, Seattle: University of Washington Press.

Emmelhainz, Irmgard (2019), 'Decolonial love', *E-Flux Journal*, 99, pp. 1–6.

Escobar, Arturo (2022), 'Global higher education in 2050', *Critical Times*, 5:1, pp. 183–201, https://doi.org/10.1215/26410478-9536551.

Everett-Green, Robert (2018), 'Is virtual reality about to break through as an artists' medium?' *The Globe and Mail*, 9 June, https://www.theglobeandmail.com/arts/art-and-architecture/article-canadian-artists-lead-the-way-in-realizing-the-artistic-promise-of-vr/. Accessed 17 March 2025.

Farman, Jason (2018), *Delayed Response: The Art of Waiting from the Ancient to the Instant World*, New Haven: Yale University Press, https://doi.org/10.12987/9780300240726.

Fenelon, James and Alford, Jennifer (2020), 'Envisioning Indigenous models for social and ecological change in the Anthropocene', *Journal of World-Systems Research*, 26:2, pp. 372–99, https://doi.org/10.5195/jwsr.2020.996.

Findling, John E. and Pelle, Kimberly D. (1990), *Historical dictionary of world's fairs and expositions*, 1851–1988, New York: Greenwood Press.

Forni, Silvia and Cipolla, Craig (2022), 'Miss Chief in the Museum: Of Legends, Science, Stories, and Truths', in *Kent Monkman: Being legendary*, Toronto: Art Canada Institute, pp. 166–171.

Forrest, Michelle, McCullagh, Suzanne, Reilly, Ian, (2024), 'Feminist Reading Together in a Different Register', *Studies in Social Justice*, 18, pp. 721–741. https://doi.org/10.26522/ssj.v18i4.4290

Fournier, Lauren (2021), *Autotheory as Feminist Practice in Art, Writing, and Criticism*, Cambridge, MA: MIT Press.

Frase, Peter (2016), *Four Futures: Life After Capitalism*, London: Verso Books.

Freelon, Deen, Pruden, Meredith L., Eddy, Kristen A. and Kuo, Rachel (2023), 'Inequities of race, place, and gender among the communication citation elite, 2000–2019', *Journal of Communication*, 73:4, pp. 356–67, https://doi.org/10.1093/joc/jqad002.

Fricke, Suzanne Newman (2019), 'Indigenous futurisms in the hyperpresent now', *World Art*, 9:2, pp. 107–21, https://doi.org/10.1080/21500894.2019.1627674.

Fuchs, Christian and Fuchs, Claudia (2022), 'De-colonising academia: A radical humanist perspective', in C. Fuchs (ed.), *Digital Humanism*, Bingley: Emerald Group Publishing Limited, pp. 63–110.

Fujikane, Candace (2021), *Mapping Abundance for a Planetary Future: Kanaka Maoli and Critical Settler Cartographies in Hawai'i*, Durham, NC: Duke University Press.

Furtado, Nicole (2024), 'Indigenous futurisms', in B. Mark, B. Andrew and V. Sherryl (eds), *The New Routledge Companion to Science Fiction*, 2nd ed., London: Routledge, pp. 26–33.

Gaonkar, Dilip Parameshwar (2002), 'Toward new imaginaries: An introduction', *Public Culture*, 14:1, pp. 1–19, https://doi.org/10.1215/08992363-14-1-1.

Glossary (n.d.), documenta fifteen, https://documenta-fifteen.de/glossar/. Accessed 17 March 2025.

Glück, Antje (2018), 'De-westernization and decolonization in media studies', in *Oxford Research Encyclopedia of Communication*, Oxford: Oxford University Press, https://doi.org/10.1093/acrefore/9780190228613.013.898.

Gómez-Barris, Macarena, (2017), *The Extractive Zone: Social Ecologies and Decolonial Perspectives*, Durham, NC: Duke University Press.

Gongora, Romeo (2022), *Awaken Dreams: Decolonising Participatory Art Through Communal Friendship*, London: Goldsmiths, University of London, https://doi.org/10.25602/GOLD.00032056.

Graeber, David (2018), *Bullshit Jobs*, New York: Simon & Schuster.

Graham, Mark, Ojanperä, Sana and Dittus Martin (2014), 'Internet geographies: Data shadows and digital divisions of labor,' in M. Graham and W. Dutton (eds), *Society and the Internet: How Networks of Information and Communication are Changing Our Lives*, Oxford: Oxford University Press, pp. 99–116.

Gray, Jonah (2017), 'Wood land school: A brief report', *Wood Land School: A Brief Report*, 133, pp. 12–18.

Greenfield, Adam (2017), *Radical Technologies: The Design of Everyday Life*, London: Verso Books.

Greenhalgh, Paul (1988), *Ephemeral Vistas: The Expositions Universelles, Great Exhibitions, and World's Fairs, 1851-1939*, Manchester, NH: Manchester University Press.

Grosfoguel, Ramón (2007), 'The epistemic decolonial turn: Beyond political-economy paradigms', *Cultural Studies*, 21:2&3, pp. 211–23, https://doi.org/10.1080/09502380601162514.

Haiven, Max and Khasnabish, Alex (2014), *The Radical Imagination: Social Movement Research in the Age of Austerity*, London: Zed Books.

Hall, Martin (2015), 'The symbolic statue dividing a South African university', *BBC News*, 25 March, https://www.bbc.com/news/business-31945680. Accessed 17 March 2025.

Hampton, John and the Wood Land School (2017), 'Wood Land School Goes to Documenta: A Discussion on Indigenous Institutional Critique, Part 2', *Canadian Art*, 31 August, https://canadianart.tempurl.host/features/wood-land-school-documenta. Accessed 17 March 2025.

Hanchey, Jenna N. (2022), 'Afrofuturist lessons in persistence', in S. Blithe and J. C. Bauer (eds), *Badass Feminist Politics: Exploring Radical Edges of Feminist Theory, Communication, and Activism*, New Brunswick: Rutgers University Press, pp. 276–91

Haraway, Donna J. (2016), *Staying with the Trouble: Making Kin in the Chthulucene*, Durham, NC: Duke University Press.

Hardawar, Devindra (2018), 'The surprising beauty of nature reclaiming Toronto in VR', *Engadget*, 20 April, https://www.engadget.com/2018-04-20-biidaaban-vr-tribeca.html. Accessed 17 March 2025.

Harjo, Laura (2019), *Spiral to the Stars: Mvskoke Tools of Futurity*, Tucson: University of Arizona Press.

Harvey, Penny (1996), *Hybrids of Modernity: Anthropology, the Nation State and the Universal Exhibition*, London: Routledge.

Hayes, Aneta, Luckett, Kathy and Misiaszek, Greg (2021), 'Possibilities and complexities of decolonising higher education: Critical perspectives on praxis', *Teaching in Higher Education*, 26:7&8, pp. 887–901, https://doi.org/10.1080/13562517.2021.1971384.

Hill, Gord (2010), *500 Years of Indigenous Resistance*, 2nd ed., Oakland: PM Press.

Hirji, Faiza, Jiwani, Yasmin and McAllister, Kristen Emiko (2020), 'On the margins of the margins: #CommunicationSoWhite – Canadian style', *Communication, Culture and Critique*, 13:2, pp. 168–84, https://doi.org/10.1093/ccc/tcaa019.

Hoffenberg, Peter H. (2001), *An Empire on Display: English, Indian, and Australian Exhibitions from the Crystal Palace to the Great War*, Berkeley: University of California Press.

Hogan, Mél (2018), 'Big data ecologies', *Ephemera*, 18:3, pp. 631–57.

Hollenbach, Julie (2023), 'The seeds of an orange: Meditations on reverberations and cultural sovereignty in the Craftwork of Tyshan Wright', in *A Handmade Assembly*, Sackville: Struts Gallery, pp. 46–55, https://www.strutsgallery.ca/product-page/a-handmade-assembly.

Howe, Stephen (2002), *Empire: A Very Short Introduction*, Oxford: Oxford University Press.

Hult, Anna (2013), 'Swedish production of sustainable urban imaginaries in China', *Journal of Urban Technology*, 20:1, pp. 77–94, https://doi.org/10.1080/10630732.2012.735405.

Igloliorte, Heather, Jim, Alice Ming Wai, Morton, Erin, Nelson, Charmaine A., Nighttraveller, Cheli, Ripley, Aj, Taunton, Carla, Vukov, Tamara, Cahill, Susan and Holmes, Kristy A. (2017), 'Killjoys, academic citizenship and the politics of getting along', *TOPIA: Canadian Journal of Cultural Studies*, 38, pp. 187–208, https://doi.org/10.3138/topia.38.187.

Iyer, Usha (2022a), 'A pedagogy of reparations', *Feminist Media Histories*, 8:1, pp. 181–93, https://doi.org/10.1525/fmh.2022.8.1.181.

Iyer, Usha (2022b), 'Smuggling, infiltrating, usurping: Why globalizing the film and media studies curriculum is essential to decolonizing it', *Journal of Cinema and Media Studies*, 61:6, https://quod.lib.umich.edu/cgi/t/text/idx/j/jcms/18261332.0061.602/--smuggling-infiltrating-usurping-why-globalizing-the-film.

Jasanoff, Sheila (2015), 'Future imperfect: Science, technology, and the imaginations of modernity', in J. Sheila and K. Sang-Hyun (eds), *Dreamscapes of Modernity: Sociotechnical Imaginaries and the Fabrication of Power*, Chicago: University of Chicago Press, pp. 1–33.

Johnson, Rhiannon (2017), 'ImagineNATIVE VR imagines Indigenous lives in 150 years', *CBC News*, 20 October, https://www.cbc.ca/news/indigenous/imaginenative-virtual-reality-1.4365311. Accessed 17 March 2025.

Johnson, Rhiannon (2018), 'Anishinaabe artist's new VR experience takes an Indigenous futurist look at Toronto', *CBC News*, 14 April, https://www.cbc.ca/news/indigenous/lisa-jackson-biidaaban-vr-future-toronto-1.4619041. Accessed 17 March 2025.

Juneja, Monica and Ziebritzki, Jo (2023), 'Learning with documenta 15: Principles, practices, problems', *Grey Room*, 92, pp. 94–105, https://doi.org/10.1162/grey_a_00380.

Kabatay, Jasmine (2019), 'Indigenous virtual reality experience heading to Wilfrid Laurier's Brantford Campus', *CBC News*, 22 January, https://www.cbc.ca/news/canada/hamilton/indigenous-virtual-reality-experience-heading-to-wilfrid-laurier-s-brantford-campus-1.4986812. Accessed 17 March 2025.

Kassam, Ashifa (2018), 'Trans Mountain pipeline halted after Canadian court overturns approval', *The Guardian*. 30 August, https://www.theguardian.com/world/2018/aug/30/trans-mountain-pipeline-latest-canada-court-overturns. Accessed 17 March 2025.

Kauffman, Emma (2023), 'Prefiguring an Abolitionist University: To be in but not of', *TOPIA*, 47, pp. 180–88, https://doi.org/10.3138/topia-2023-0011.

Keet, André (2019), 'The plastic university: Knowledge, disciplines and the decolonial turn', in J. Jansen (ed.), *Decolonisation in Universities: The Politics of Knowledge*, Johannesburg: Wits University Press, pp. 202–16.

Kenneally, Rhona Richman and Sloan, Johanne (2010), 'Introduction: Dusting off the souvenir', in R. Kenneally and J. Sloan (eds), *Expo 67*, Toronto: University of Toronto Press, pp. 1–24, https://doi.org/10.3138/9781442660205-003.

Kentgens, Simon and Cramer, Florian (2023), *Lumbung, Commons and Community Art*, HumDrumPress, https://humdrumpress.com/Lumbung. Accessed 17 March 2025.

Khoo, Su-ming and Vered, Anique (2020), 'Including the "invisible middle" of decoloniality', *Journal of International Women's Studies*, 21:7, pp. 225–42.

Kimmerer, Robin (2013), *Braiding Sweetgrass: Indigenous Wisdom, Scientific Knowledge and the Teachings of Plants*, Minneapolis: Milkweed Editions.

Kinder, John B. (2021), 'Solar infrastructure as media of resistance, or, Indigenous solarities against settler colonialism', *South Atlantic Quarterly*, 120:1, pp. 63–76, https://doi.org/10.1215/00382876-8795718.

King, Thomas (2012), *The Inconvenient Indian: A Curious Account of Native People in North America*, Toronto: Doubleday Canada.

King, Tiffany Lethabo, Navarro, Jenell and Smith, Andrea (2020), 'Beyond incommensurability: Toward an otherwise stance on black and Indigenous relationality', in T. L. King, J. Navarro and A. Smith (eds), *Otherwise Worlds: Against Settler Colonialism and Anti-Blackness*, Durham, NC: Duke University Press, pp. 1–24, https://doi.org/10.1515/9781478012023-001.

Knight, Chris (2018), 'How Biidaaban imagines a future in which the First Peoples have reclaimed their territory', *National Post*, 21 September, https://nationalpost.com/entertainment/movies/how-biidaaban-imagines-a-future-in-which-the-first-peoples-have-reclaimed-their-territory.

Köhler, Benedikt, David, Sabria and Blumtritt, Jörg (2010), *The Slow Media Manifesto*, https://en.slow-media.net/manifesto.

Kwon, Diana (2022), 'The rise of citational justice: How scholars are making references fairer', *Nature*, 603:7902, pp. 568–71, https://doi.org/10.1038/d41586-022-00793-1.

Land, Clare (2015), *Decolonizing Solidarity: Dilemmas and Directions for Supporters of Indigenous Struggles*, London: Zed Books.

Lau, Charlene K. (2022), 'Before yesterday we could fly: An Afrofuturist period room', *Journal of Curatorial Studies*, 11:2, pp. 234–37, https://doi.org/10.1386/jcs_00072_7.

Lettau, Meike and Canyürek, Özlem (2024), 'Epistemological shifts, power imbalances and conflicts at documenta fifteen: Decolonial cultural policy conceptions beyond Eurocentric universalism', *International Journal of Cultural Policy*, 31:2, pp. 1–18, https://doi.org/10.1080/10286632.2024.2316101.

Levin, Miriam R. (2021), 'What were world's fairs for? Catalysts for trade-based urban development in the Second Industrial Revolution', *Journal of Urban History*, 47:6, pp. 1203–24, https://doi.org/10.1177/0096144220913301.

Lewis, Jason Edward (2016), 'A brief (media) history of the Indigenous future', *Public*, 27:54, pp. 36–50, https://doi.org/10.1386/public.27.54.36_1.

Liboiron, Max (2021), *Pollution is Colonialism*, Durham, NC: Duke University Press.

Lim, Audrea (2020), 'Has Trudeau (politely) betrayed native people again?' *New York Times*, 10 March, https://www.nytimes.com/2020/03/10/opinion/canada-natives-pipeline.html. Accessed 17 March 2025.

Lim, Merlyna (2018), 'Roots, routes, and routers: Communications and media of contemporary social movements', *Journalism & Communication Monographs*, 20:2, pp. 92–136, https://doi.org/10.1177/1522637918770419.

Lindström, Kristina and Ståhl, Åsa (2020), 'Living with', in K. Jungnickel (ed.), *Transmissions: Critical Tactics for Making and Communicating Research*, Cambridge, MA: MIT Press, pp. 131–51.

Linklater, Duane, Lukin Linklater, Tanya, turions, cheyanne, and Scott, Walter (2017), *Wood Land School: Kahatenhstánion tsi na'tetiatere ne Iotohrkó:wa tánon Iotohrha Drawing Lines from January to December*, SBC galerie d'art contemporain, https://www.sbcgallery.ca/wood-land-school-fr?lang=en. Accessed 17 March 2025.

Loveless, Natalie (2019), *How to Make Art at the End of the World: A Manifesto for Research-Creation*, Durham, NC: Duke University Press.

Lukin Linklater, Tanya (2017), 'Desirous kinds of Indigenous futurity: On the possibilities of memorialization', in H. Davis (ed.), *Desire Change*, Montreal: McGill-Queen's University Press, pp. 149–62.

Lumbung (n.d.), documenta fifteen, https://documenta-fifteen.de/en/lumbung/. Accessed 17 March 2025.

Machado de Oliveira, Vanessa (2021), *Hospicing Modernity: Facing Humanity's Wrongs and the Implications for Social Activism*, Berkeley: North Atlantic Books.

Madianou, Mirca (2025), *Technocolonialism: When Technology for Good Is Harmful*, Cambridge: Polity Press.

Mafile'o, Tracie, Kokinai, Clare Wedu and Redman-MacLaren, Michelle (2022), 'We story: Decoloniality in practice and theory', *Cultural Studies ↔ Critical Methodologies*, 22:6, 547–61, https://doi.org/10.1177/15327086221105666.

Maldonado-Torres, Nelson (2007), 'On the coloniality of being: Contributions to the development of a concept', *Cultural Studies*, 21:2&3, 240–70, https://doi.org/10.1080/09502380601162548.

Martineau, Jarrett and Ritskes, Eric (2014), 'Fugitive indigeneity: Reclaiming the terrain of decolonial struggle through Indigenous art', *Decolonization: Indigeneity, Education & Society*, 3:1, pp. i–xii.

Marx, Karl and Engels, Friedrich (1970), *The German Ideology*, C. J. Arthur (ed.), New York: International Publishers.

Marx, Karl (2008), *Capital: An Abridged Edition*, David McLellan (ed.), Oxford: Oxford University Press.

Mattern, Shannon (2020), 'The spectacle of data: A century of fairs, fiches, and fantasies' *Theory, Culture & Society*, 37:7&8, pp. 133–55, https://doi.org/10.1177/0263276420958052.

Maynard, Robyn and Simpson, Leanne Betasamosake (2022), *Rehearsals for Living*, Chicago: Haymarket Books.

Mbembe, Achille (2019), 'Future knowledges and their implications for the decolonisation project', in J. Jonathan (ed.), *Decolonisation in Universities: The Politics of Knowledge*, Johannesburg: Wits University Press, pp. 239–54.

McDonough, Tom (2010), 'Obsolescence as progress and regression: Technology, temporality, and architecture at Expo 67', in K. Rhona Richman and S. Johanne (eds), *Expo 67*, Toronto: University of Toronto Press, pp. 83–92.

McGinn, Dave (2017), 'Indigenous artists create virtual-reality vision of a future Canada', *The Globe and Mail*, 22 June, https://www.theglobeandmail.com/arts/indigenous-artists-create-virtual-reality-vision-of-canada-in-the-future/article35436268/. Accessed 17 March 2025.

Media Space (2018), 'Biidaaban: First Light', https://mediaspace.nfb.ca/epk/biidaaban/. Accessed 17 March 2025.

Meighan, Paul J. (2021), 'Decolonizing the digital landscape: The role of technology in Indigenous language revitalization', *AlterNative: An International Journal of Indigenous Peoples*, 17:3, pp. 397–405, https://doi.org/10.1177/11771801211037672.

Mergler, Agata (2022), 'documenta fifteen and Berlin Biennale 12: A comparative review', *NECSUS European Journal of Media Studies*, 11:2, pp. 340–58.

The Met (2021), 'Before yesterday we could fly: An Afrofuturist period room virtual opening', YouTube, https://www.youtube.com/watch?v=A_1QbBQ5pag. Accessed 17 March 2025.

Michell, B., Toledano, M. and Wickham, J. (dir) (2024) *Yintah*. EyeSteelFilm. [Online Documentary] https://www.yintahfilm.com.

MIT Open Documentary Lab _Docubase (2018), 'Biidaaban: First Light', https://docubase.mit.edu/project/biidaaban-first-light/. Accessed 17 March 2025.

Mignolo, Walter D. (2002), 'The geopolitics of knowledge and the colonial difference', *South Atlantic Quarterly*, 101:1, pp. 57–96, https://doi.org/10.1215/00382876-101-1-57.

Mignolo, Walter D. (2009), Epistemic disobedience, independent thought and decolonial freedom, *Theory, Culture & Society*, 26:7&8, pp. 159–81, https://doi.org/10.1177/0263276409349275.

Mignolo, Walter D. (ed.) (2021a), 'Delinking, decoloniality, and de-westernization', in *Delinking, Decoloniality, and De-Westernization*, Durham, NC: Duke University Press, pp. 314–48.

Mignolo, Walter D. (2021b), *The Politics of Decolonial Investigations*, Durham, NC: Duke University Press.

Mignolo, Walter D. and Walsh, Catherine E. (2018), *On Decoloniality: Concepts, Analytics, Praxis*, Durham, NC: Duke University Press.

Miller, Sara Cedar (2022), *Before Central Park*, New York: Columbia University Press.

Mitchell, Audra and Chaudhury, Aadita (2020), 'Worlding beyond "the" "end" of "the world": White apocalyptic visions and BIPOC futurisms', *International Relations*, 34:3, pp. 309–32, https://doi.org/10.1177/0047117820948936.

Moffitt, Evan (2023), 'Kent Monkman unmasks the colonial complicity of museums', *ArtReview*, 23 January, https://artreview.com/kent-monkman-unmasks-the-colonial-complicity-of-museums-being-legendary-royal-ontario-toronto-review/. Accessed 17 March 2025.

Monkman, Kent and Gordon, Gisèle (2022), *Kent Monkman: Being Legendary*, Toronto: Art Canada Institute.

Monkman, Kent and Gordon, Gisèle (2023a), *The Memoirs of Miss Chief Eagle Testickle: A True and Exact Accounting of the History of Turtle Island, Vol. one*, Toronto: McClelland & Stewart.

Monkman, Kent and Gordon, Gisèle (2023b), *The Memoirs of Miss Chief Eagle Testickle: A True and Exact Accounting of the History of Turtle Island, Vol. two*, Toronto: McClelland & Stewart.

Moore, Sylvia (2017a), 'Strengthening all our relations', *Engaged Scholar Journal*, 2:1, pp. 287–96, https://doi.org/10.15402/esj.v2i1.211.

Moore, Sylvia (2017b), *Trickster Chases the Tale of Education*, Montreal: McGill-Queen's University Press.

Moran, Padraig (2024), 'Haida Gwaii's future, Haida Gwaii's past', *The Current*, 9 September, https://www.cbc.ca/i/phoenix/player/syndicate/?mediaId=9.6504332.

Mosco, Vincent (2004), *The Digital Sublime: Myth, Power, and Cyberspace*, Cambridge, MA: MIT Press.

Mosco, Vincent (2014), *To the Cloud: Big Data in a Turbulent World*, New York: Paradigm Publishers.

Moten, Fred and Harney, Stefano (2020), *The university (last words)*, https://www.academia.edu/43580248/The_university_last_words_by_stefano_harney_and_fred_moten. Accessed 17 March 2025.

Moyo, Last (2020), *The Decolonial Turn in Media Studies in Africa and the Global South*, Cham: Springer International Publishing, https://doi.org/10.1007/978-3-030-52832-4

Moyo, Last (2024), *Cultural Policy and Cultural Industries in Africa: From Culture as a Commodity to Culture as Praxis*, Cham: Springer International Publishing, https://doi.org/10.1007/978-3-031-57742-0.

Mullaney, Thomas S., Peters, Benjamin, Hicks, Mar and Philip, Kavita (eds) (2020), *Your Computer Is on Fire*, Cambridge, MA: MIT Press.

Murphy, Timothy (2015), 'Ally is action, not an identity', *HuffPost*, 12 November, https://www.huffpost.com/entry/ally-is-action-not-an-identity_b_8536518. Accessed 17 March 2025.

Mussett, Ben (2022), 'A day at Kent Monkman's studio', *The Globe and Mail*, 23 September, https://www.theglobeandmail.com/arts/art-and-architecture/article-a-day-at-kent-monkmans-studio. Accessed 17 March 2025.

Natale, Simone and Balbi, Gabriele (2014), 'Media and the imaginary in history: The role of the fantastic in different stages of media change', *Media History*, 20:2, pp. 203–18, https://doi.org/10.1080/13688804.2014.898904.

Ndlovu-Gatsheni, Sabelo J. (2018), 'Rhodes must fall', in S. J. Ndlovu-Gatsheni (ed.), *Epistemic Freedom in Africa: Deprovincialization and Decolonization*, London: Routledge, pp. 221–42.

Ndlovu-Gatsheni, Sabelo J. (2023), 'Beyond the coloniser's model of the world: Towards reworlding from the Global South', *Third World Quarterly*, 44:10, pp. 2246–62, https://doi.org/10.1080/01436597.2023.2171389.

Nelson, Charmaine A. (2017), '"Ran away from her master … a negroe girl named Thursday": Examining evidence of punishment, isolation, and trauma in Nova Scotia and Quebec fugitive slave advertisements', in E. Morton (ed.), *Unsettling Canadian Art History*, Montreal: McGill-Queen's University Press, pp. 160–78.

Newell, Sasha and Pype, Katrien (2021), 'Decolonizing the virtual: Future knowledges and the extrahuman in Africa', *African Studies Review*, 64:1, pp. 5–22, https://doi.org/10.1017/asr.2020.88.

Ng, Eve, White, Khadijah Costley and Saha, Anamik (2020), '#CommunicationSoWhite: Race and power in the academy and beyond', *Communication, Culture and Critique*, 13:2, pp. 143–51, https://doi.org/10.1093/ccc/tcaa011.

Nguyen, Clinton (2016), '7 unsuccessful World's Fair inventions that predicted future technology', *Business Insider*, 13 June, https://www.businessinsider.com/7-worlds-fair-inventions-that-predicted-future-technology-2016-6. Accessed 17 March 2025.

Nixon, Lindsay (2020), 'Visual cultures of Indigenous futurism', in T. Lethabo King, J. Navarro and A. Smith (eds), *Otherwise Worlds: Against Settler Colonialism and Anti-Blackness*, Durham, NC: Duke University Press, pp. 332–42, https://doi.org/10.1215/9781478012023-022.

Noam, Eli M. (2016), *Who Owns the World's Media?: Media Concentration and Ownership Around the World*, Oxford: Oxford University Press.

Nordin, Astrid (2012), 'Space for the future: Exhibiting China in the world at the Shanghai Expo', *China Information*, 26:2, pp. 235–49, https://doi.org/10.1177/0920203X12438000.

Notes from America with Kai Wright (2023), 'How Afrofuturism Redefines Our Past', WNYC Studios, New York, 2 January, https://www.wnycstudios.org/podcasts/anxiety/episodes/how-afrofuturism-redefines-our-past. Accessed 17 March 2025.

Odell, Jenny (2019), *How to Do Nothing: Resisting the Attention Economy*, Brooklyn: Melville House.

Olito, Frank (2019), '15 inventions and landmarks that you had no idea debuted at World's Fairs', *Insider*, 18 July, https://www.insider.com/inventions-debuted-at-worlds-fairs-2019-7. Accessed 17 March 2025.

Pandey-Kanaan, Aastha (2024), 'B.C. signs agreement handing over title to Haida Gwaii', *CityNews Vancouver*, 15 April, https://vancouver.citynews.ca/2024/04/15/bc-signs-lands-agreement-haida-gwaii. Accessed 17 March 2025.

paperson, la (2017), *A Third University Is Possible*, Minneapolis: University of Minnesota Press.

Pérez, Laura Elisa (2019), *Eros Ideologies: Writings on Art, Spirituality, and the Decolonial*, Durham, NC: Duke University Press.

Perry, Imani (2018), *Vexy Thing: On Gender and Liberation*, Durham, NC: Duke University Press.

Petit, Yann (2023), '*The African Origin of Civilization* by Alisa LaGamma and Diana Craig Patch, and: *Before Yesterday We Could Fly: An Afrofuturist Period Room* by Hannah Beachler et al. (review)', *African Arts*, 56:1, pp. 89–91, https://www.muse.jhu.edu/article/882198.

Philip, Kavita (2021), 'The internet will be decolonized', in T. S. Mullaney, B. Peters, M. Hicks and K. Philip (eds), *Your Computer Is on Fire*, Cambridge, MA: MIT Press, pp. 91–116.

Pierce, Joseph M. (2024), 'A true and exact history of queer Indigenous sovereignty', *Hyperallergic*, 11 March, http://hyperallergic.com/876430/kent-monkman-gisele-gordon-true-and-exact-history-of-queer-indigenous-sovereignty/. Accessed 17 March 2025.

The Proclamation—Alcatraz Occupation 1969 (n.d.), 'Rising: The American Indian Movement and the Third Space of Sovereignty', https://muscarelle.wm.edu/rising/alcatraz/proclamation/. Accessed 17 March 2025.

Puig de la Bellacasa, Maria (2017), *Matters of Care: Speculative Ethics in More than Human Worlds*, Minneapolis: University of Minnesota Press.

Quijano, Aníbal (2007), 'Coloniality and modernity/rationality', *Cultural Studies*, 21:2&3, pp. 168–78, https://doi.org/10.1080/09502380601164353.

Quinn, Patrick (2022), 'Kent Monkman's "being legendary" exhibit at the ROM', *Penticton Herald*, 2 November, https://www.pentictonherald.ca/spare_news/article_a584d03e-5db2-5096-bb55-c40fc0074484.html. Accessed 17 March 2025.

Rattan, Chris (2018), 'Virtual reality film imagines an Indigenous future for Toronto', *NOW Toronto*, 14 September, https://nowtoronto.com/culture/virtual-reality-film-imagines-an-indigenous-future-for-toronto. Accessed 17 March 2025.

Rauch, Jennifer (2018), *Slow Media: Why 'Slow' Is Satisfying, Sustainable, and Smart*, Oxford: Oxford University Press.

Regembal, Eléa (2017), 'Resistance through gathering', *The McGill Daily*, 13 November, https://www.mcgilldaily.com/2017/11/resistance-through-gathering/. Accessed 17 March 2025.

Rice, Ryan (ed.) (2002), 'Presence and absence: Indian art in the 1990s', in *Définitions de la culture visuelle V: Mondialisation et postcolonialisme*, Montréal: Musée d'art contemporain de Montréal, pp. 96–103.

Risam, Roopika (2022), 'Indigenizing decolonial media theory', *Feminist Media Histories*, 8:1, pp. 134–64, https://doi.org/10.1525/fmh.2022.8.1.134

Ritchie, Laura (2022), 'Sobey Art Award 2022: Tyshan Wright', 4 November, https://www.gallery.ca/magazine/exhibitions/sobey-art-award-2022-tyshan-wright. Accessed 17 March 2025.

Rivera Cusicanqui, Silvia (2020), *Ch'ixinakax utxiwa: On Decolonising Practices and Discourses*, Cambridge: Polity Press.

Roche, Maurice (2000), *Megaevents and Modernity: Olympics and Expos in the Growth of Global Culture*, London: Routledge.

Rose-Antoinette, Ronald (2018), 'Backdoor of the world', *Flash Art*, https://flash--art.com/article/backdoor-of-the-world/. Accessed 17 March 2025.

Roy, Arundhati (2020), 'The pandemic is a portal', *Financial Times*, 3 April, https://www.ft.com/content/10d8f5e8-74eb-11ea-95fe-fcd274e920ca. Accessed 17 March 2025.

ruangrupa (2022), *documenta fifteen Handbook*, Berlin: Hatje Cantz.

ruangrupa Selected as Artistic Direction of documenta fifteen (2019), *documenta fifteen*, https://documenta-fifteen.de/en/press-releases/ruangrupa-selected-as-artistic-direction-of-documenta-fifteen/. Accessed 17 March 2025.

Rydell, Robert W. (1984), *All the World's a Fair: Visions of Empire at American International Expositions, 1876-1916*, Chicago: University of Chicago Press.

Rydell, Robert W. (1993), *World of Fairs: The Century-of-Progress Expositions*, Chicago: University of Chicago Press.

Sacred Earth Solar, 'Our Projects', https://sacredearth.solar/our-projects. Accessed 15 May 2025.

Sandals, Leah (2016), 'Indigenous artists to reimagine Canada's future in VR', *Canadian Art*, 21 June, https://canadianart.ca/news/indigenous-artists-reimagine-canadas-future-vr/. Accessed 17 March 2025.

Santos, Boaventura De Sousa (2018), *The End of the Cognitive Empire: The Coming of Age of Epistemologies of the South*, Durham, NC: Duke University Press.

Schmelzer, Matthias, Vetter, Andrea and Vansintjan, Aaron (2022), *The Future is Degrowth: A Guide to a World Beyond Capitalism*, London: Verso Books.

Sharma, Sarah (2014), *In the Meantime: Temporality and Cultural Politics*, Durham, NC: Duke University Press.

Shipley, Tyler A. (2020), *Canada in the World: Settler Capitalism and the Colonial Imagination*, Halifax: Fernwood Publishing.

Shotwell, Alexis (2016), *Against Purity: Living Ethically in Compromised Times*, Minneapolis: University of Minnesota Press.

Shulruff, Toby and Wyman, Levi (2023), 'A trip through Tomorrowland: The World Expo as futures lab', *World Futures Review*, 15:1, pp. 22–37 https://doi.org/10.1177/19467567231151718

Silverstone, Roger (1999), *Why Study the Media?*, London: Sage.

Simpson, Audra (2014), *Mohawk Interruptus: Political Life Across the Borders of Settler States*, Durham, NC: Duke University Press.

Simpson, Leanne Betasamosake (2011), *Dancing on Our Turtle's Back: Stories of Nishnaabeg Re-creation, Resurgence and a New Emergence*, Winnipeg: Arbeiter Ring Publishing.

Simpson, Leanne Betasamosake (2014), 'Land as pedagogy: Nishnaabeg intelligence and rebellious transformation', *Decolonization: Indigeneity, Education & Society*, 3:3, pp. 1–25.

Simpson, Leanne Betasamosake (2017), *As We Have Always Done: Indigenous Freedom Through Radical Resistance*, Minneapolis: University of Minnesota Press.

Simpson, Leanne Betasamosake (2021), *A Short History of the Blockade: Giant Beavers, Diplomacy, and Regeneration in Nishnaabewin*, Edmonton: University of Alberta Press.

Singh, Julietta (2017), *Unthinking Mastery: Dehumanism and Decolonial Entanglements*, Durham, NC: Duke University Press.

Skawennati (2015), 'Imagining the next seven generations', YouTube, 16 July, https://www.youtube.com/watch?v=kDDOWF31WpI. Accessed 17 March 2025.

Skura, Elyse (2016), '2167: Indigenous artists to use virtual reality to imagine Canada's future', *CBC News*, 23 June, https://www.cbc.ca/news/canada/north/2167-indigenous-virtual-reality-art-project-1.3647580. Accessed 17 March 2025.

Smith, Janet (2019), 'With sprawling transmissions, Lisa Jackson creates a new film language from Indigenous roots', *The Georgia Straight*, 28 August, https://www.straight.com/arts/1292826/sprawling-transmissions-lisa-jackson-creates-new-film-language-indigenous-roots. Accessed 17 March 2025.

Smith, Linda Tuhiwai (2021), *Decolonizing Methodologies: Research and Indigenous Peoples*, 3rd ed., London: Zed Books.

Soper, Kate (2020), *Post-growth Living*, London: Verso Books.

Speed, Shannon (2017), 'Structures of settler capitalism in Abya Yala', *American Quarterly*, 69:4, pp. 783–90.

Srinivasan, Ramesh (2019), *Beyond the Valley: How Innovators Around the World are Overcoming Inequality and Creating the Technologies of Tomorrow*, Cambridge, MA: MIT Press.

Srnicek, Nick (2017), *Platform Capitalism*, Cambridge: Polity Press.

Srnicek, Nick and Williams, Alex (2016), *Inventing the Future: Postcapitalism and a World Without Work*, London: Verso Books.

Steeves, Paulette (2022), 'Indigenous Histories: We Come From the Stars', in *Kent Monkman: Being Legendary*, Toronto: Art Canada Institute, pp. 52–55.

Stephenson, Amanda (2022), 'Cost of Trans Mountain pipeline expansion soars 70% to $21.4 billion', *CBC News*, 18 February, https://www.cbc.ca/news/canada/calgary/trans-mountain-pipeline-expansion-calgary-1.6357174. Accessed 17 March 2025.

Stevenson, Matt (2018), '25 years ago, AT&T predicted the future we're living now', *Wired*, 25 November, https://www.wired.com/brandlab/2018/11/25-years-ago-att-predicted-future-living-now/. Accessed 17 March 2025.

Stewart, Michelle (2023), 'The generative hope of Indigenous interactive media: Ecological knowledge and Indigenous futurism', in D. Claxton and E. Winton (eds), *Indigenous Media Arts in Canada: Making, Caring, Sharing*, Waterloo: Wilfrid Laurier University Press, pp. 289–316.

Stewart-Ambo, Theresa and Yang, K. Wayne (2021), 'Beyond land acknowledgment in settler institutions', *Social Text*, 39:1, pp. 21–46.

Stoltz, Pauline, Mulinari, Diana and Keskinen, Suvi (2021), 'Contextualising feminisms in the Nordic region: Neoliberalism, nationalism, and decolonial critique', in S. Keskinen, P. Stoltz and D. Mulinari (eds), *Feminisms in the Nordic Region*, Cham: Springer International Publishing, pp. 1–21, https://doi.org/10.1007/978-3-030-53464-6_1.

Sundar, Pavitra and Mukherjee, Debashree (2022), 'Editors' introduction', *Feminist Media Histories*, 8:1, pp. 1–15, https://doi.org/10.1525/fmh.2022.8.1.1.

Taffel, Sy (2023), 'Data and oil: Metaphor, materiality and metabolic rifts', *New Media & Society*, 25:5, pp. 980–98, https://doi.org/10.1177/14614448211017887.

Taylor, Carol A. (2020), 'Slow singularities for collective mattering: New material feminist praxis in the accelerated academy', *Irish Educational Studies*, 39:2, pp. 255–72, https://doi.org/10.1080/03323315.2020.1734045.

Taylor, Charles (2004), *Modern Social Imaginaries*, Durham, NC: Duke University Press.

Thorat, Dhanashree (2019), 'Colonial topographies of internet infrastructure: The sedimented and linked networks of the telegraph and submarine fiber optic internet', *South Asian Review*, 40:3, pp. 252–67, https://doi.org/10.1080/02759527.2019.1599563.

Tiny House Warriors (2017), 'Solar Panels in the Path of a Pipeline!' https://www.facebook.com/tinyhousewarriors/videos/solar-panels-in-the-path-of-a-pipeline/190479251513904. Accessed August 6, 2025.

Treuer, David (2019), 'How a native American resistance held Alcatraz for 18 months', *New York Times*, 20 November, https://www.nytimes.com/2019/11/20/us/native-american-occupation-alcatraz.html. Accessed 17 March 2025.

Truth and Reconciliation Commission of Canada. (2015), *Final Report of the Truth and Reconciliation Commission of Canada*, Toronto: James Lorimer and Company Ltd. Publishers.

Tsing, Anna (2015), *The Mushroom at the End of the World: On the Possibility of Life in Capitalist Ruins*, Princeton: Princeton University Press.

Tuck, Eve and Gaztambide-Fernández, Rubén A. (2013), 'Curriculum, replacement, and settler futurity', *Journal of Curriculum Theorizing*, 29:1, pp. 8–34.

Tuck, Eve and Yang, K. Wayne. (2012), 'Decolonization is not a metaphor', *Decolonization: Indigeneity, Education & Society*, 1:1, pp. 1–40.

turions, cheyanne (2017), 'How not to install Indigenous art as a feminist', in H. Davis (ed.), *Desire Change: Contemporary Feminist Art in Canada*, Montreal: McGill-Queen's University Press, pp. 242–56.

Vázquez, Rolando (2020), *Vistas of Modernity: Decolonial Aesthesis and the End of the Contemporary*, Amsterdam: Mondriaan Fund.

Walsh, Catherine E. (2020), 'Decolonial learnings, askings and musings', *Postcolonial Studies*, 23:4, pp. 604–11, https://doi.org/10.1080/13688790.2020.1751437.

Walsh, Catherine E. (2023), *Rising Up, Living On: Re-Existences, Sowings, and Decolonial Cracks*, Durham, NC: Duke University Press.

Weeks, Kathi (2011), *The Problem with Work: Feminism, Marxism, Antiwork Politics, and Postwork Imaginaries*, Durham, NC: Duke University Press.

Weisman, Alan (2007), *The World Without Us*, New York: Harper Perennial.

Wemigwans, Jennifer (2018), *A Digital Bundle: Protecting and Promoting Indigenous Knowledge Online*, Regina: University of Regina Press.

Wemigwans, Jennifer and Sharma, Sarah (2022), 'Toward a media theory of the digital bundle: A conversation with Jennifer Wemigwans', in S. Sharma and R. Singh (eds), *Re-Understanding Media*, Durham, NC: Duke University Press, pp. 208–24.

Whyte, Kyle (2017), 'Our ancestors' dystopia now: Indigenous conservation and the Anthropocene', in U. Heise, J. Christensen and M. Niemann (eds), *The Routledge Companion to the Environmental Humanities*, London: Routledge, pp. 222–31.

Whyte, Murray (2017), 'imagineNATIVE gathers dark VR visions of the future', *Toronto Star*, 17 October, https://www.thestar.com/entertainment/visual-arts/imaginenative-gathers-dark-vr-visions-of-the-future/article_f196601d-226f-5e76-b0f3-b3721be7c18d.html. Accessed 17 March 2025

Wilson, Kate (2019), 'Indigenous VR experience Biidaaban imagines Toronto after reconciliation', *The Georgia Straight*, 9 January, https://www.straight.com/tech/1185526/indigenous-vr-experience-biidaaban-imagines-toronto-after-reconciliation.

Wilson, Sheena (2018), 'Energy imaginaries: Feminist and decolonial futures', in B. R. Bellamy and J. Diamanti (eds), *Materialism and the Critique of Energy*, Chicago: MCMPrime Press, pp. 377–412.

Winseck, Dwayne (2022), *Media and Internet Concentration in Canada, 1984–2021*, Ottawa: Canadian Media Concentration Research Project, http://www.cmcrp.org/3569-2/. Accessed 17 March 2025.

Wolfe, Patrick (2006), 'Settler colonialism and the elimination of the native', *Journal of Genocide Research*, 8:4, pp. 387–409, https://doi.org/10.1080/14623520601056240.

yamomo, meLê and Beyer, Theresa (2024), '"Framing Europe" – meLê yamomo interviewed by Theresa Beyer', in C. Grüny and B. Farnsworth (eds), *New Music and Institutional Critique*, Berlin: Springer Berlin Heidelberg, pp. 195–205.

Yates, Julian S. (2020), 'On decoloniality ... and the "decolonial problem"', *Postcolonial Studies*, 23:4, pp. 589–95, https://doi.org/10.1080/13688790.2020.1751433.

Yintah (2024), Directed by Brenda Michell, Michael Toledano, and Jennifer Wickham. [Documentary film]. EyeSteelFilm.

Index

Page numbers in italics indicate black and white figure; colour figures are referenced by *col figs* followed by page numbers in italics; Page numbers followed by n represents notes in the text.

www.ingramcontent.com/pod-product-compliance
Lightning Source LLC
LaVergne TN
LVHW070945150726
842928LV00004B/7
* 9 7 8 1 8 3 5 9 5 3 5 8 7 *